Paths to Immortality Based on the Undeniable Powers of Human Nature

Johann Baptist Krebs

Paths to Immortality Based on the Undeniable Powers of Human Nature

Johann Baptist Krebs

translated by Kerry A Nitz

K A Nitz
AUCKLAND, NEW ZEALAND

Wege zur Unsterblichkeit
auf unläugbare Kräfte der menschlichen Natur
published in German c.1855
under the pseudonym J. Kernning

This translation into New Zealand English
Copyright © K A Nitz 2023
All rights reserved

ISBN: 978-0-473-67896-8

Table of Contents

Translator's Note..7
Foreword..9
Introduction..11
The Scholar..35
The Image of the Beloved..37
The Doppelganger..43
Ruppert's Family..49
Continuation of the Oral Instruction..................................73
The Shaft..81
The New Heaven..91
Comparisons with the Bible..93
Overview...109
About the Author..119

Translator's Note

For the English translation of Bible texts I have made use of the King James Version. Where I thought it would be helpful I have also inserted missing Biblical citations in the footnotes.

The author's somewhat idiosyncratic approach to presenting dialogue has also been retained.

Regarding the names of the key characters, it is worth noting that *Silber* is German for silver, and *Mohr* is the German noun for Moor (as in Othello, not as in uncultivated land).

Foreword

Immortality is the highest goal of humanity. As much as has already been written about this subject, the importance of the matter demands again and again new instruction and encouragement so that we are constantly reminded to not let our only true possession out of our sight.

Wherever we look connections are seen for which the ordinary outer life does not suffice, and we only find the fulfillment which the soul yearns for in the certain prospect of eternity. It is suspected that the knowledge of religion does not suffice if it is not exercised in practice, hence it is placed under the laws of an association in order to thereby as it were force yourself to offer your sacrifice to eternity and obtain claims to it.

Not to everybody is it begrudged to find such associations where the laws of eternity are derived from basic truths and brought into use, hence the author has made it his task to consider human nature in its knowable effects, and to use the phenomena of the latter as the first foundation for his composition.

Eternity is everywhere. Anyone who can recognise eternity already has a certain right to be eternal themselves; it is thus mainly about humanity coming to a proper recognition and preparing them through this for eternity. From this point of view, life obtains a new form because everything then only has value for it when it also gives it security for the future, even for eternity.

Theories are of no use anymore in our day and age because we please ourselves too much in the ability of making knowledge; we make the means into the goal, and thereby lose the crown of our existence.

The goal is immortality, the means to it are knowledge and feelings. When we boast about knowledge and wallow in feelings to pass the time, we remain standing before the door to the house, and rejoice at the beautiful exterior whilst the furnishings inside remains unknown to us.

Immortality is our goal. I have assembled how to achieve and to recognise it, and am passing on to my colleagues how I received it as a picture of nature where all the contours are given, and have connected the parts often only with effort to the whole.

But the result will show whether the task is solved. If even only a few accept the teaching, then already a great thing has happened; but I wish to give all humanity the conviction of an eternal duration, because in that lies not only a happy outlook for the future, but also strength and composure for the storms of the present.

In this sense and with this wish, I hand over this little work to receptive hearts who, not entirely carried away by the present, still make time to yearn for eternity in order to bring to fruition what they have sown here, and find in the feeling of imperishability strength and courage to separate the eternal from the temporal, and to give to everybody what they deserve.

The author.

Introduction

The path to immortality is not as easy to find as you would imagine. There are indeed many paths, but precisely because of that many become doubtful and think that whatever can be reached in such various ways does not need any rule and is found in the end by itself. We see the so-called educated world in this belief almost without exception, and this treatise is especially composed for them. But even others who have taken the safer road on the path to belief will find a strengthening of their views, and thereby become clearly conscious of their feelings, obtaining still more strength for their life path.

Immortality is the peak of human perfection, and the doctrine over it shall be treated on this basis because you can more easily climb a steep rise by means of ordered steps. But since a system would be too dry and only be of use to a smaller portion of the readers, it is considered expedient to clothe the matter in historical examples in which the principles are connected with the practice and thereby become understandable for everybody.

In order to characterise all the more faithfully the key persons by which this goal shall be achieved and to describe their life views all the more precisely, the author has retained a part of their correspondence over the present subject without any alteration; only where the exercise begins and demands verbal impartation is the form of narration chosen.

The exchange of letters presents itself between two acquaintances: Fielding and Silbert. The former, son of a government official, showed from his youth onward a great partiality for metaphysics. In Göttingen he got to know a theosophist who initiated him into all the secrets of that science, and demonstrated that humanity possesses the ability to become as certain of their immortality as they are in control of the use of their outer senses. For a profession he had studied economics, and had occupied for twenty years the post of a lord's steward on a large estate.

Silbert was the son of wealthy parents and lived in the capital as a lawyer. Since he did not see the need to take on every legal dispute for the sake of money, he followed his urge to look into all branches of human knowledge, and finally hit upon the doctrine of the immortality of humanity. He read everything which had been written about this important topic, but did not find the enlightenment which he sought, and turned therefore to his old university friend, Fielding, of whom it was said that he was well informed on this point.

The latter undertook to share his views and experiences with him, but found such a spirit of contradiction in the student that he felt compelled to lead him through all the aberrations of the human spirit, as it were through a labyrinth, in order to place him in the standpoint where it would be possible for him to recognise the truth.

We will pass over the previous relations of the persons concerned because they do not relate to the matter, and begin at the moment when Silbert expressed his wish to Fielding to receive some instruction in the immortality of humanity.

***

Fielding to Silbert

You desire from me information about the nature of humanity and describe this desire with the expression: paths to immortality.

You are right. Anyone who knows the path to immortality also has information about the nature of humanity; for humanity and immortality are mutually dependent, just as the ability to fly is contained in the concept "bird".

Two views reign over immortality, of which by necessity only one can be the correct one. According to the first, all humans are without exception immortal. According to the second, they possess the ability to struggle for such a thing.

To the first class belongs the great crowd who would like to possess the goods without making much of a sacrifice for it. Humans bristle at the second view because they surely see that, if it comes to the struggle, something would have to happen which is contrary to their desires and habits.

Introduction

From this you will see how difficult it is to describe exactly the path to immortality, because we do not know yet whether we have not already strolled along it, or whether there is reason to strike out on a different path.

Humans are called to immortality, that is, they are capable of living for eternity if they fulfil the conditions which are necessary for drawing themselves out of the darkness by which they are surrounded.

For the present, I know nothing more to say to you. Perhaps this will suffice to lead you onto the trail on which you can stroll with easy steps to immortality.

***

Silbert to Fielding

Thank you for putting the effort in to answer my letter. I have previously already thought about the matter, but not found *one* concise principle which could have served me as a signpost for further inquiries. Now a small light has been given to me in that I have seen that humans do not obtain such easy purchase on the highest good which the creator can give creatures, immortality. "They must struggle," you say, "must fulfill conditions to which they are subjected by the laws of nature." But what are these laws? Who discerns them? I do not indeed doubt in the immortality of humans, but the present and given means do not appear sufficient to me for obtaining it. Hence I must take up your generosity and ask you to show me thorough — I would like to say — new paths which will lead me to the conviction and the realisation of my task.

You see what a burden you have imposed on yourself in that you have gotten involved in the answering of my doubts; but I hope by your patience and thoroughness that you will not stop yourself from teaching me, even if you find me deeper in confusion than you perhaps suspected.

***

Johann Baptist Krebs

Fielding to Silbert

Your writing caused me a restless day. With your confession that you considered all present means for immortality to be insufficient, the history of our time passed by me, where anyone feels called to think and to speak about eternal laws which they like and which agree with their current circumstances; I saw the fruitlessness of our knowledge, our learned institutions and colleges, which indeed gave us some things to digest, but did not teach the precious jewel, what can become of humans, the certainty of our life.

You must allow already that I, in order to become more comprehensible, will strike out a little far, and express myself over the worth of faith in specifics, as well as in general.

In our days, I know, you mock the word "faith" because you do not believe it has any power, thinking yourself by contrast to be at the peak of all knowledge where you do not need such feelings anymore. Only, in order to consider our task in its first buds, it is necessary that you stroll with me on the path of faith until it becomes for you a certainty or a source of knowledge.

Faith is a foundation pillar of ennobled human nature. By it the human steps into a new sphere and obtains something which all knowledge cannot give him: view into eternity. All instruction which we can give about immortality must lead first of all to faith, because without this we have no firm ground for any sort of guarantee.

Faith is based in human nature, like thinking and feeling. The simple, uncorrupted human finds himself drawn to it as his own life goal; this feeling is in this way animated in him so that he possesses without it no grounds either for the momentary or still less for an eternally continued existence. He and eternity are related, and if the latter is contained in any one thing, then it belongs to his nature because he experiences in himself the basic material of everything eternal.

I am convinced that if you think about your career then you will bump up against an epoch where the thought of eternity was your greatest happiness, where you, full of pious emotions, yearned only for fulfillment of your suspicions and satisfaction of the innermost urges of your soul. That was the time of your life's flowering; a pity that the frost came over it and destroyed the buds in their development. Now you must prepare a new spring in your heart, and with manly power of belief preserve the blossoms so that a ripe fruit comes from them, then the path to immortality which you have lost and I shall show you is found again.

***

Silbert to Fielding

Accept my honest thanks for the shimmer of light which you showed me so amiably. You shifted me back to the years of my youth where I found myself in heaven in my parents' circle and thought of nothing else at all but angels and saints for eternity and myself under them. Oh, that those dreams had to vanish! But they were only dreams, hence they could not stay. It was the time of roses in my life, the spring, as you say; the leaves fell, and as the rose brings forth no fruit, so too with the youthful emotion of faith. Summer comes in its scorching atmosphere, the shimmer flees, and in unveiled truth the image of death shows itself. The events of the world touch us, the admonition of time calls us into the outer life, we must take an interest, must be active, show our powers, struggle, wrestle, and establish ourselves as a peculiar whole which itself gives itself its contours and laws. How can the delicate germ of faith exist there? Where would it find a place to form only a little branch, much less a crown?! I feel it more and more: humans must not rise too high in their hopes, they are merely the builder's labourer of this earth; when they have completed their day's work, they step away in order to make another place. 'Good!', they say when they have done their work, then step away in order to receive their reward. Here is the partition wall which separates the utopians from the truth and sends the faithful into dreams of whose disappearance they dare not think.

Reward! What is reward! — Pleasure! Does life give us pleasures? — Countless. We see the brilliance of creation, feel the delights of love, choose and determine at will, and enthral ourselves in our deeds; all the senses seem only present so as to spice the life and to make every moment of it a heaven for us! Ear and eye, taste, smell, and feeling unite to beautify our existence and to reward us for the smidgen of effort which we sacrifice for our needs. How can we make yet further claims for reward? Have we not already received it in abundance? — Here you will indeed counter: the worries, struggles and fears, sicknesses, pains and persecutions, even the constant fear of death, are not things which are to be enjoyed by a passing pleasure; for this a retribution must follow, which is of the higher sort in order to establish the equilibrium again. Such expressions do not seem without basis, and the importance of them appears to us powerfully; but with closer illumination they vanish again into nothing. From where do most illnesses, persecutions, and evil arise? Is not the human himself for the most part guilty of them? If he lived simply, compatibly and in accord with nature, then he would be healthy, free, and happy! Nature is just! It has given the reward in advance to those who want to receive it; only those who push it away stubbornly and unlovingly live in want amidst immeasurable wealth.

This, dear friend, is my life view, my confession of faith. I certainly see well that it robs me of much of the pleasure of the soul which is accorded to those who connect their happiness with eternity, and I envy the plain townsman when he visits church with inner devotion and fancies himself in heaven there; but the consideration that I live in a carefree manner whilst he has to struggle with sweat and toil for himself and his family, and in the thoughts of a reward on the other side receives it in the here and now already, that produces the equilibrium perfectly.

***

Fielding to Silbert

Your confession of faith, which actually excludes all faith, is a sort of philosophy where the human abandons himself and prepares for himself in the concoction of others an uncomfortable residence. The natural love for the better self has been lost in you; you are in raptures in the outer world, and hence you must have concepts and ideas for all your life experiences. Concepts and ideas, however, belong only in part

Introduction

to us ourselves because we usually receive them from others, and process them in the given forms within ourselves. The secure property of the human are his feelings, and every judgement which does not proceed from this or lead back to it again is uncertain and and leaves us in the lurch when embarrassments happen. On this basis you will not become impatient if I yet make an attempt to penetrate into your heart in order to awaken a spark there which will lead us onto the desired path.

The word "faith" is contrary to your way of thinking. This expression, which describes a high power of humanity, is too far gone and in part signals incorrectly that we feel ourselves ever under the dominion of an authority when we devote ourselves to it; hence, in order to wander along the entered path, it is necessary to make use of another word which has almost the same interpretation.

Religiosity is the tree on which the fruit of faith grows. It is the life power which involuntarily reminds the human of eternity, of a creator, and which only those entirely captive to prejudices are able to deny. At no time and under no stretch of heaven was this urge entirely suppressed; indeed, we also observe that, in the past as in the present, on all islands and parts of the world where the power of creation develops into human form, we meet religious customs which occupy themselves with the other side, with eternity and immortality. Whether and to what extent all these customs achieve the goal is not to be investigated here because we want merely to convince ourselves of the presence of the urge which leads to it.

Religiosity is the original basis of all morals and virtues. Without the indestructible inkling of an eternal life, morals and virtues would be the mere sound of words, without worth or necessity. From it comes the feeling of honour, decorum, shame, friendship, loyalty, love, duty, in one word everything which ennobles humanity and can raise it to a free, spiritual existence. It is the shield which secures humanity from complete degeneration, which emerges victorious from every darkness, from all political and religious struggles, and again shows humans the paths for grounding their lives and for the veneration of the creator.

I point to this characteristic of humanity, and if you are capable of finding the same in yourself, then you are standing at the same point to which I was willing to lead you to by faith, and are entering the certain path to immortality.

***

Silbert to Fielding

Because faith bears no fruit in me, you offer me religiosity. I find indeed that this feeling is far more comprehensive than the former, but from whatever side I look at it, for my way of thinking it is not enough. Religiosity is in my view the presentiment of an eternal dominion which stands over the affairs of the world and orders them on the whole.

When I consider the confusion which reigns for the most part in human affairs, the necessity of such an uppermost referee who lights up the darkness in which we hover becomes palpable. But whether this judge also takes care of the eternal permanence of the individual as well as the whole is a question which no feeling can answer.

The human must learn to think, his highest life power consists of that. He must never be dominated by feelings when reason is speaking. This invites him to a free expression of power which originates from consideration and shows us the area of activity. Reason loses itself in limitation and isolation because it lacks the ideas; in generality, however, it strengthens itself with every new action until finally the whole becomes clear for it. Religiosity belongs to those alone who possess it, they can explain it to nobody nor share it with anyone; the works of reason by contrast are able to spread and are thereby common goods of all humanity. Now where is the higher goal? What is most conducive to the human and thereby for humanity? The ennoblement of humanity is our task, and the greater the extent to which this is fulfilled, the higher we stand on the steps to perfection.

It understandable in itself that such an activity cannot be expressed without struggles and friction. Parties form, opinions oppose one another, and advocate their matter with effort and jealousy, for life and death. These are the necessary outpourings of a general striving for happiness and truth which must in the end spread amongst humanity. What use could religiosity be in such an agitation? How could it exist in the disputes of contending parties? It is a tender plant on the battlefield which you trample without noticing. It is a flower on the broad road, covered in dust, and crushed by the foots of the wayfarers without them seeing its beauty or smelling its balsam air. I must compare it to a child in a world of giants who opposes in vain the attacks of their rough environment. Religiosity is indeed more than faith, because it could serve in case of need as the foundation for a system; but it cannot give anything positive either, because it arises from feelings which themselves have no enduring certainty.

***

Fielding to Silbert

The content of your writing thwarted the greatest part of my expectations. I had prepared for obstinacies, but did not think that they would be so overarching and methodical. You deprive faith of all strength! Religiosity is to you a weak child amongst giants! How am I then to penetrate into your heart and thereby use it to defeat the mind if such powers have no impact?

Human nature is indeed rich in feelings which stem from eternity, but not all are suited to making immortality clear for us. But I want to make another attempt and hope that this will not miss the mark because it touches the basic power of our entire existence. So listen! — If you cannot trust and hand yourself over to any of the feelings I named for you, then you will be yet true though to the love for yourself, for your own life! — The love for life is indestructible and never vanishes, neither in the turmoil of the world, nor in the struggles of parties. It is the belt which binds us to ourselves; it invites us without end to blow up the gates of eternity and to seek a path to immortality. Anyone who loves their life, esteems and acknowledges themselves in it, they cannot bear the thought of an eternal death, and so strive at any price for a means of preserving themselves and vaulting over the putrefaction.

Life or death lie before us. Anyone who loves only the appearance of life, but not life itself, has not yet recognised it and might fritter it away in comfortable ease; but you must not stand still anymore, you must walk the path and even if I should lead you through thorns. Hence I give you this last suggestion for consideration and hope that your heart tires of the oppression, that it shall apply itself to its lost rights again.

***

Silbert to Fielding

Dear friend! The patience with which you suggest one means after the other to me in order to vanquish my obstinate urge to doubt is worthy of admiration, and I consider it almost unscrupulous to put your kindness further to the test with new objections. Only, since I have once made a start of disclosing my views, you will forgive me if I continue to reveal my most secret thoughts, and to show you what an enormous work you undertook when you made the decision to win me over to the belief in immortality. But back to the matter at hand.

Because in me the tenderer feelings have died, you seek to grasp me by the root of all life urges, by the love for life. I must confess, there cannot be a more undeniable and more general power than the urge to preserve one's life; only even this feeling is no lever for immortality anymore with us cosmopolitans, because we esteem the efficacy and the shimmer of life higher than life itself. I believe I have understood you fully — you think that the consciousness that I live should suffice for me and provide a replacement for all the lack of an imperfect working; indeed, you seem to put forward the principle that anyone has only themselves to satisfy in order to gratify all their hopes and wishes. Anyone who is capable of that — I suspect — has found themselves and does not need the swirling dance of the world anymore; but precisely this drawing back into oneself, this dissociation from all which sets our powers into action, is to my eyes like a living death which is yet more terrible than complete annihilation. If I must no longer be active, must not work anymore for others and on others, then I find life to be aimless and the love for it vanishes to the degree that I withdraw from others. Can I also rely on myself in this state, and reckon on success, provide the strength for a new life course? No, truly no! I am not capable of thinking of such a dissociation being possible, and if you are not in a position to give me yet another guide, then immortality remains for me a hypothesis in whose dissection only vain wordy philosophy can boast.

According to your views, the world stands in a perverse direction; it has placed its entire worth on outer activity, instead of inner activity. Why does one allow that to happen? Why did the wise, who were always present, not hold humanity back from the false path? Then it would be easy to obey our feelings because we would not know anything else, and the happiness of the forest dweller would be no chimera for us; but now, when the history of the past and present is coming to fruition, when events and reforms have become needs for us, now the time is past when everybody was enough in themselves and only found in the calm of their hearts the goal and the gratification of their existence.

The world, one certainly says, has not changed, the old eternally recurs. I cannot get used to such and other sayings. Humanity must have its childhood, its youth, and its maturity. It is not yet mature, I confess it myself, but in the process of an eternal striding forwards, and hence the past cannot serve us as a pattern for the present. Where formerly nomads roamed, civilisation now reigns; where the rough power of the fist asserted itself, law rules, and hence humans must leave the forest and enter into society with their fellows in order to instruct them and be instructed by them.

This and other cosmopolitan ideas have so obtained the upper hand in me that I consider it impossible to ever free myself of them and not recognise them to be true.

**

Fielding to Silbert

It would be pointless for me to get involved in the refutation of your life views because your heart and mind are bound up with and have become one with them. I must still just offer as much that the perversion cannot be driven any higher than in our days where everybody seeks to act as guardian over the others, and neither the guardian nor the patronised stands on their own powers. The oak can develop itself, the lion feels its strength through its nerves, but the human has sunk down to the delusion that nature is too stingy towards him, and had only given him alone no positive powers and no innate growth. The human has like any other creature his peculiar stamp; when he does not blur this, he gets to know nature and himself. But when he loses it, then he can indeed play with words and expressions learnt by rote, but he will obtain no sparks of pure knowledge and truth. The truth of humanity is based on the consciousness of immortality! This consciousness, however, is not to be learnt through book learning; indeed, rationalism has itself no single tenable basis for the eternal permanence of humanity, and hence we must, if the human contains the highest law of human nature in himself, renounce immortality straightaway. You see what seriousness the matter obtains when we consider it exactly; for you see yourself compelled to throw down the gauntlet to almost the entire civilised world and to say to it that it is in error. — If you are still determined after this explanation to get some clarity about our task, it will be expedient to spend some time in my vicinity, because mere propositions are of no avail anymore, but instead it becomes necessary to proceed to the practice. My duties do not allow me to visit you, but it will be an easy thing for you to sever yourself from your cases and hand them over for the time being to another. I therefore look forward to your imminent arrival, and you shall be as well served by me as is only ever possible in the countryside.

***

Silbert with Fielding
(oral instruction)

Silbert immediately made preparations after receipt of that last letter to go away for some time. Since his duties were not collegial, it was not difficult to dispose of them and on the fourth day he arrived at Fielding's in H...ld. The latter received him with warmth, placed him in a pleasant room, and said, "It is good that you are visiting me! Letters are not capable of much with you, I hope oral instruction will succeed instead in bringing you some certainty."

Introduction

"You had the kindness," Silbert replied, "to illuminate my doubt with rare patience. Even if I do not yet stand at the point which can gratify you, I am relying on your magnanimity again and expect instruction from you in a matter which, if it can be acknowledged with conviction, will be of the greatest benefit for me."

Fielding offered him his hand and said, "Are you challenging me? Well now, it's accepted! I will make the attempt to lead you to the conviction. On the other hand, I desire from you courage and persistence; for the path which must be shown to such a doubter as you are is rough and passes through all the bends of life." — "I will be steadfast," Silbert said, "will you instruct me as to what I have to do?" — "To remain calm," Fielding responded, "and let yourself be purified a little by the country air, then opportunity will be found to speak about what should happen."

Silbert accepted that. He visited the nearby places, saw the curiosities of the area, and spent a week in this way on constant strolls. On the ninth day, as both were sitting together after lunch and talking about the affairs of their fatherland, Fielding made the remark, "Germany is a great meadow, rich in grass, but as a result poorer in flowers which would be worthy of being transferred to a garden."

Silbert: From where does that come?

Fielding: Each strives to stand out amongst the grasses as grass; nobody may raise themselves to flower, out of fear of standing alone.

Silbert: I note where you are aiming! The cosmopolitan mind is not much good at your way of thinking! You desire exceptions.

Fielding: Exceptions? Well now; I wish to give each the courage to be independent and to enter that class where the higher human nature sets its banner.

Silbert: Amidst the crowd you miss this?

Fielding: Amidst the crowd it cannot develop because the interests thwart each other too much.

Silbert: Therefore a dissociation is necessary?

Fielding: Yes. In all ages humanity was separated into two classes, where the one sought only the form, but the other the nature in the form.

Silbert: That claim is new.

Fielding: Nothing less — the Bible expresses it distinctly before and after the Flood, in that it separates humanity into children of God and the children of men. Christ also called the latter the dead, and the former children of light or of life.

Silbert: And from this division you deduce the proof for immortality?

Fielding: If the division shows itself to be true, then the proof follows by itself.

Silbert: Quite right! But how is this truth recognised?

Fielding: There are two basic proofs for immortality. Firstly, the prophetic power which looks into the future and instructs us about the situation after death. The second arises from the contacts with the dead who deliver us the apparent proof of their continuation.

Silbert: It would be immodest of me to speak out against such proofs, for I must assume that they have been demonstrated because you refer to them with such certainty. I ask only on which of these two paths I shall arrive at the conviction?

Fielding: On the second.

Silbert: Why not on the first?

Fielding: Because it would not suffice for you. The prophetic power expresses itself so naturally that the doubter is easily tempted to ascribe an accidental coincidence to what the divination previously announced.

Silbert: But if it foretells unusual things?

Fielding: That doesn't make a difference, because we also see unusual phenomena in the outer world.

Silbert: Thus you point me to the dead? How shall I reach them? How can I make the impossible possible?

Fielding: What others have achieved is not impossible for you and anyone who possesses persistence and courage. I desire only your resolve.

Silbert: My resolve? You astound me, show me the means, then I will try it.

Fielding: The means shall be yours.

Silbert: Truly? Well, then take my promise.

Fielding: Your hand on it?

Silbert: Here it is.

Introduction

Fielding: It has happened. The life behind you must vanish in order to make another place. Welcome from me to your new life course!

Fielding was called away. Silbert remained alone and felt in a strange mood. He had examined many branches of human knowledge with thoroughness, he could not think of any possibility of a passing over to the dead. Were Fielding, he thought, not so certain in other things, then I would consider him to be a fool who laboured under a fantasy; but I must remain silent and wait and see the result.

After a few days they strolled through a field in which several types of fruit and other plants were germinating which Fielding had had delivered from other lands and was trialling here. This gave them cause to speak about the richness of the plant world, about the driving force of nature, and finally about the variety of all things which in the main, however, stood again in the greatest similarity.

"The laws are eternal," Fielding remarked, "hence the agreement."

Silbert: But the types disappear!

Fielding: In terms of form, yes, but their being can continue under given conditions.

Silbert: What are these conditions?

Fielding: From all stones and plants a spiritual element, a spiritus can be drawn which remains past decomposition.

Silbert: If that is so, then the basic matter for immortality lies in the human, and nothing is needed but the drawing of this imperishable phoenix to the light and preserving it from the retiring into the night.

Fielding: You are right. But precisely both these tasks are not easy to be solved. As many wander through life and do not find this phoenix; with others by contrast it has already begun its development, but they do not heed their own and they let it vanish again unneeded.

Silbert: That is what always plunges me into new doubt. Nature has is original materials, these are unalterable and eternal. What is the primal power of the human spirit? Does it possess features which may be merely acknowledged in order to be convinced of its eternal permanence?

Fielding looked at him apprehensively and said, "You are giving your doubts ever new nourishment in order to make the path to conviction difficult. A short time ago it seemed enough for you to seek the imperishable phoenix and now you desire already to know the primal power of which it consists. Well now! Let us just once analyse creation in its basic parts and see what results follow from it."

"The first thing we see is the earth. It is that about which, according to the senses, everything turns and acts on. If the movement of the stars in the heavens might happen according to another system, for our observation the sensory visible one is the correct one. The earth is the receptacle into which the upper powers lower their procreative rays and call forth everything which in creation reveals itself in colour, form, movement, and activity. It is the mother who conveys everything to the light, who provides each of her children with the stamp of the father and sends it on its destiny. In the earth we see the first basic matter which bears imperishability in itself."

"After this the plants reveal themselves to us. They originate by a sort of procreation in the earth; then they climb towards the light, grow, sprout flowers, and finally fruit. The plant kingdom is by its nature not a primary kingdom because it is lacking the maternal power. The human appears here as handmaid, sows, plants, grafts according to free will. In the same field he places lilies and roses, strews seed, inserts stakes, and everything must develop in its way as the human considers appropriate for his use. He works here like a small creator in the great creation and makes entire regions subservient to himself. The earth is to him for this goal the mother in which he places his embryos so that they develop and come to the light."

"Above the plant kingdom, a higher one is revealed to us, the realm of life. Here we step into the area where we no longer perceive the powers by our senses, but rather can only derive them from their effects on our being. Life is a primal power which builds from earth a house, a body, encloses itself in it as mother and touches itself with influences from above, creates and reproduces itself."

Introduction

"The animal kingdom has countless gradations; but for the observer it decomposes into only two main classes: into toneless creatures, and into such as with which one or several sounds can be perceived. The former are closer to the plant kingdom, but the latter open for us already the outlook on a higher form in that we perceive with them characteristic feelings and an instinct similar to thought."

"Standing above the animals is the human who brings all his feelings to consciousness and describes them with names. In him are all the sounds and powers of life. The thought, as primal power, penetrates into him, and raises him to maternal dignity in that it awakes in him the germ of knowledge which grows and produces the fruits of faith and conviction."

"Three kinds of humans impose themselves on the researcher and form thereby just as many subdivisions."

"Firstly, such as are extremely simple, raising themselves only a little above the feelings, and deciding mechanically in language learnt by rote and performing just as mechanically. These are living clockwork mechanisms which are wound up by commands, habits, or even by a teacher, and continue for as long as the cord exists on the weights."

"Secondly, such as in which the power of comparison is awoken and unlocks for them a particular field of activity. To these the present is too narrow, they penetrate into the past, research the history of all peoples and search for the agreement or the variance of those with our time. Language gives them means for new forms of thinking with which they test the correctness or falsity of all judgements and phenomena. Arts and sciences blossom here because the feelings are brought to knowledge and these are modified by that. This class are described by the wise ones with the expression: 'the world'. It is the realm which threatens to swallow everything; in it there is the dominance over humanity, without caring whether this may also happen according to the law of truth. — I need not say anything further to you over it, you know it well enough."

"Thirdly, such as who withdraw from all that is given and turn their eyes merely to nature and the eternal truth in order to be instructed by this over the basic purpose of life. Here a new sphere enters into the education of humanity. They abandon the narrow limits of temporality, step across into the realm of the eternal paternal power, and let this pass creatively into themselves, from which a new, an inner human arises who draws all the life powers towards the centre, and prepares thereby an eternal duration for the human. In this state all the outer law-making and learnedness stops for humans; they have come to the source from which all knowledge and accomplishments flow; they stand, new philosophers, above the crowd, consistent with themselves, and give drinks to those who approach them with thirst and beg them for refreshment."

"Over all these primal powers and subdivisions reigns God, who is and fulfills everything that is connected to the primal powers of his might and is therefore imperishable, in eternal efficacy without struggle, in uninterrupted clairvoyance without deception, resting on his own majesty from eternity to eternity!"

"This is a short outline of nature. If you develop an understanding of it, then it has the good property that it distances you from one-sidedness and shows you the ways of creation. Without practice, however, all contemplation is aimless and leads only into new labyrinths."

Fielding fell silent here and observed the impression which this analysis of creation had made on his friend. He left him with the words, "Deliberate on what we discussed, I have still a few matters to deal with; we will meet again at the dinner table."

Silbert remained alone in thought and sought to fix in his memory the given sequence of steps in order perhaps to be able to ascend them later on all the quicker. "It is the seventh step*," he said to himself, "on which he thought to place me; from there I shall look across at those preceding and ask them about the conditions of immortality."

Three days passed before he could speak again about this topic with his friend. On the fourth Fielding visited him in the room, and made the suggestion to him that he accompany

---

* [Tr.: i.e. the third type of human, after earth, plants, animals (two types), and the first two types of human.]

Introduction

him to a village two hours away in order to get to know one of his friends there.

Silbert: What use can a new acquaintance be to me when I am not yet straight over what you have said to me?

Fielding: That will be revealed. Four eyes see more than two and a witness to my instruction could strengthen your courage.

Silbert: I do not need any witness — I place complete trust in you. If I yet doubt, then this is doubt of myself and of the possibility of ever reaching the seventh step you described.

Fielding: You will reach it; my word on that. Only the how is not yet clear to me and hence the assistance of a friend would be welcome to me.

Silbert: Not to me. Leave me here until I am more certain of my case; then I will not resist hearing from a second mouth the same lecture perhaps only with different pictures. Just answer me a few questions instead.

Fielding: I am listening.

Silbert: At what stage does immortality begin?

Fielding: It begins nowhere, for it is always there.

Silbert: The earth does not live and therefore cannot die. But if it had life, would it last for eternity?

Fielding: We do not want to argue over words. The earth is primal material and hence eternal.

Silbert: And plants?

Fielding: They are a created mixture and hence perishable.

Silbert: Could you not claim thus just as well for animals and humans too?

Fielding: Oh yes.

Silbert: Then you contradict your own doctrine.

Fielding: What I said also affects the animal kingdom in terms of form. To the extent, however, that life is primal material, it cannot perish.

Silbert: Animals thus have eternal duration?

Fielding: If it can salvage its ego, yes! Since it is lacking the means for that, however, its life flows back into the eternal primal current, and the earth turns again to earth.

Silbert: Now and humans?

Fielding: They can become lords of their ego.

Silbert: With what means?

Fielding: The simple ones learn to believe and to love, and reproduce themselves.

Silbert: And worldly people?

Fielding: Depends on their constitution, on their learnedness, on brilliance and honour, on untiring activity, on thousands of concerns, fears, and distractions. They live with time and pass in time.

Silbert: But on the seventh step there is certainty of life?

Fielding: There infallibly.

Silbert: How do you obtain it?

Fielding: You penetrate through the mist. You form in yourself a core of light which draws all light to itself and pushes away from itself the coarse. The sun nourishes itself in that it takes up all the light matter from the surrounding planets and gathers the purest light in its centre. In the sun the rays go inwards and not outwards. The human must become like that, the capability is within him. If his ego is found in the purest light of life, in the centre, then it cannot perish anymore, but instead must last for as long as God and nature remain connected with it.

Silbert: I cannot counter your words with anything anymore. The doubts flee, but I lack the ability to take up the truth in myself. Give me this, take me on as student and lead me to the goal.

Fielding: Right, then hear the teacher's words: go back to your work, but come back in five months and learn to think during this time in your inner being the little word "I".

Now the task had been pronounced. Silbert, who had expected unfamiliar sentences and deeply hidden truths in artificially set syllogisms, could not hide his astonishment. But Fielding did not let himself be deterred and continued, "You have given your word and must keep it as a man of honour. Farewell! We will see each other again in five months." He left after that and on the same day visited his friend Mohrland.

Silbert was as if turned to stone. "I shall learn to think I? I? For what? Am I then a savage who knows himself merely in his name? Shall I walk through labyrinths? I am in a labyrinth from which I see no trace of an exit! But, it is what it is, I will make the attempt. But if it does not succeed, if the task reveals itself to be a vain chimera, then I will set rigour to rigour, and set the adventurousness of this instruction in the most glaring light."

He made preparations for departure; but hesitated in this from hour to hour in the hope that Fielding would yet return. Weary of long waiting, he finally sat himself in the carriage full of wistfulness and annoyance, and travelled through the night to the capital.

He had to withstand various challenges to start with and only applied himself with reluctance to the resolution of his task. After three months it began burning in his head so that he feared he was falling ill. Only he shied from saying anything about this state to anyone, and continued his activity with a sort of defiance against himself. After five months, he called on Fielding and said, "The student comes to his strict teacher in order to account to him. I have practised my task despite reluctance and pains, have sought my ego in all parts of my body, but now find myself in the situation that I no longer know where my ego actually is. Often it occurs to me as if new senses are opening up and I see figures around me. What is that? To where does it lead? Give me information."

Fielding: You have kept your word, which pleases me. You desire information over figures which you see about yourself? I think that the person who sees something can give the most certain information. Experience is the best teacher, therefore continue your work for six more months, then it will be revealed what further work is to be done.

Silbert: I beg just the answer to one question: those figures which I see, are they beings outside me?

Fielding: What are the images of a dream?

Silbert: Pure phantoms.

Fielding: Who creates them?

Silbert: Our fantasy, our blood, our moods, and thousands of other things.

Fielding: This is the answer to your question.

Silbert: What! So there would be no spiritual contact outside of us?

Fielding: Not for the natural human. The pure spirit, however, can put itself in contact with others even over a great distance.

Silbert: That sounds so strange that I cannot get my head around it.

Fielding: The practice alone can give you clarity.

Silbert: And the figures which I see, shall I pay no attention to them?

Fielding: Who says that? I certainly do not! For the researcher the smallest thing is not too insignificant for investigation. Dream figures are images of life arisen from spiritual powers. The dreamer sees countrysides and groves, cities and villages, men and animals, strolls amongst them, makes contact with them, speaks, gets excited, works with them, rejoices and fears, loves and hates, chooses and rejects, in short, the entirety of life appears in such a perfect efficacy that he feels all the experiences of it in himself and thus truly lives. Can this be a humble ability which is capable of bringing forth everything? No, truly not! It belongs to the greatest obduracy to ignore such phenomena and not to seriously ask for once why and from where do they come.

Silbert: It is to me as if I were arriving in a new world. Always having endeavoured to consider phantoms and dream images to be useless, indeed even to be malignant products, I should obtain instruction from them.

Fielding: That is the perversity of the world which despises all spiritual phenomena and only seeks ideas or bodies. You rhapsodise with your thoughts in a heaven which you do not know and cannot reach, and on the other hand root in the earth in order to strengthen the mind. Nature shows us in dream, where our over-agitated life of the senses falls silent, spiritual shapes and thereby gives us the teaching that behind skin and flesh lives yet another life which can be active without our senses. Yes, I must voice it: dreams are for humans the first proof of a free, animated life power which takes action without our doing, and enjoys and shows itself in its own creations.

Silbert: You are drawing me ever deeper into the labyrinth instead of lighting my way.

Fielding: We must wander through labyrinths in order to find the exit to life. It lies chaotically before us and we ourselves must bring light into it. Dreams are present in order to give us the first impetus. They are the undeniable beginnings of supersensory effects which the greatest doubter cannot deny, and therefore also the safest foundation for a structure of teachings which has the knowledge of immortality for its goal. Humans are exposed too much to the sensory life, hence they can only see spiritual products in sleep. The researcher must weigh spirit and matter in the balance so that he is by free will active in both and able to make his observations, only then does he learn to distinguish what are spiritual images and what are physical images. As a result of this, however, he will obtain the historicity, even seeing awake such forms and phenomena as were previously seen in dream, and raising himself to a standpoint where he sees that the visible, physical forms are only rough, incomplete impressions of those higher, spiritual images which the opened inner senses portray. — The lowest state of spiritual life is dreaming, where the human must tolerate in himself without will the activity of good and bad spiritual powers. The highest standpoint is recognised when those powers unite with our wills and according to its laws lead us across to a spiritual activity and to an infallible clairvoyance, clairaudience, and clairsentience. Seek from that first, will-less state up to the last of the intermediary steps, and your task is resolved. You have the means; it is the previously mentioned ego. You also possess the strength, otherwise you would not yet be as advanced as you are. Stay true to your word! In half a year we will speak again about it.

He walked away. But Silbert said to himself, "Have I in dreaming heard talk of dreams, or are my senses fooled so that I see dream images when awake? I cannot get my head around it and yet I must believe; for there are dreams, who can deny this? — Dreams! — It is admittedly a wonderful state! — The human submits to incessant effort to visualise images, countrysides and lakes in artificial paintings and phantasmagorias, we praise, marvel, and idolise these dead phenomena. But in us there is a power which portrays all this animatedly and actively in great perfection; we do not pay attention to this and judge it to be a thing which seems unworthy of our attention. The human is blinded, that I see little by little; he ignores the light and seeks the night so that he will find cause to complain about darkness.

He sought out Fielding in order to take his leave. Fielding handed over to him, before he parted, a book while saying, "Here is a collection of dream, spirit, and ghost stories. Read them partly as relaxation, and in order to accustom yourself to dedicating some attention to spiritual discharges. You will frequently encounter in everyday life phenomena as you will find in this book; but you seldom get time to consider them calmly because one party nonetheless denies them with apparent truth, another though describes the same as miracles, brought about out of special considerations of the eternal omnipotence. The true researcher does not reject or believe blindly, but rather goes to the root of each phenomenon and considers it according to necessary laws. Abstain from all interpretation of whatever experiences you yourself might have. Anyone who strives constantly for meanings becomes caught and let themselves be easily led to give the interpretation more worth than the thing itself. Nature has no hieroglyphs, only real presences; those are given to the weak so that they have a guide. Recall my work with you and be assured that my wishes will constantly accompany you.

Silbert returned to the capital, practised daily for several hours and meanwhile read for relaxation the stories in the book which he had received from Fielding.

In order to lead the reader with Silbert at the same pace, we want to enclose a few of those stories here. We will keep silent about the dreams because each may have convinced themselves long ago about the truth of "being able to dream". It is not about interpretation of them here, but rather about the presence of such powers as reveal themselves through self-created images and give the human the instruction to look inside themselves and to get to know a spiritual world there.

***

The Scholar

A scholar whose name is well-known through his writings was the son of a rich craftsman. His delicate frame hindered him from continuing the profession of his father, and he also showed much talent for learning in the public high school, hence it was decided to let him study and to dedicate himself to the intellectual profession. He attended the elite high school, went on to university, and showed that he was made above all to be the most diligent and talented. In his last year at university, he wrote a book about the spheres of life, or the impact of social contact, a book which awoke great interest. Later he applied for a professorship, made a start in this post publicly as a writer, and obtained such fame as set him amongst the first of his nation. In order to avoid any bad interpretation and so as not to profane his memory, his name will kept secret here; but his story may serve as evidence of how easily humans can miss their destination and acquire characteristics which seem to remain entirely foreign to their actual nature.

He lived for thirty years in his profession as professor and as a writer with ever new intellectual products, and seemed to have already obtained the crown of his life in the here and now when an insignificant illness befell him which the doctors did not think to be at all dangerous. A light, but lasting dizziness had seized his brain, which in a short time affected his memory so much that it became difficult for him to remember everyday things. They tried everything to raise the affliction; he had to travel, distract himself, was required to neither read nor write, but it was in vain, the dizziness remained and his memory became weaker from day to day. After two years it had progressed to the point that he did not feel his affliction anymore at all, while he forgot his brilliant career completely and even lost the memory of his writings. The sight of him excited the most painful emotions; for anyone who had seen him in his work and at his intellectual prime could not comprehend how it was possible to sink down to being like a mummy. But it had happened! The scholar which he had produced in himself had died and the boy's nature made an appearance in the most garish traits.

Only now did they recall again that he had been a little joker in his youth who liked playing pranks on others, and who rejoiced when they did not surmise from where they had come. Such traits now appeared again in his behaviour quite often. What was left in his vicinity was corrupted, and when it was opportune to frighten or to surprise someone, he was inventive in taking aim; in short, the stamp of the bratty boy showed itself in his behaviour so much that it was a burden to be around him.

"Where is the spirit of this man?", some asked themselves. When you read his writings, so heart-lifting and instructive, and observed him now by contrast, you felt tempted to consider the nature of the human only to be a refined power of vegetation which briefly showed its colourful adornment in concepts, thoughts, and talk, then stripped itself, lost its crown, and crept into the arms of death.

He lived thus for over five years. His cleverness became bearishness, which finally passed into complete truculency so that he stood far below the animals. The desire to eat, which in the end completely mastered him, brought his existence, which had actually already stopped for him long ago, to an end and his memory amongst acquaintances left behind such an impression that some parents shied from dedicating their sons exclusively to the scholarly class.

***

The Image of the Beloved

In Holland the following story occurred. A ship's man by the name of Wipner had a beloved whom he had to leave when he was pressed into service as a sailor in the year 1760. Initially he was numb, and abandoned himself without thinking to the impressions of his rough company. But soon it was revealed that this did not pacify the feelings of his heart; to the contrary, amidst such wild dissipations the image of his girl appeared even more animatedly in his memory.

The ship on which he found himself received the command to set out to sea, to sail around the horn of South America, and to seek out new paths and islands in the great ocean. With dull resignation he watched the European coast vanish from his eyes — on the other side, he thought, there is no separation anymore, only there will I be happy!

In this mood he lived for three years on the ship without having set a foot on land. His behaviour was quiet, and he oversaw his duties with great punctuality so that his superiors preferred him to all others. He alone did not notice any of this, outside his duties his heart had just one feeling, to think of his beloved and dedicate himself to the hope of seeing her again soon in another world.

In the fourth year, it was right on the sixth of March, the ship lay at anchor. Wipner was sitting still on the foredeck when his eyes suddenly closed without him falling asleep, and he saw his beloved before himself. He stood up, wanted to reach out his hands to her, but she had quickly vanished. Now he sat down again, thought about the experience he had just had and said, "She has died and is coming to give me a sign of her passing over into the realm of love and happiness."

The following day he had the same experience in the same way and now he attempted to talk to her. She seemed to wave to him, but he could not hear any words. He rose, wanting to approach her, and did not see the image anymore.

It carried on in this way for several months. But now it happened so perfectly for him that he had trouble not considering it to be the person herself; she also did not vanish anymore when he approached, but rather only pulled back a specific distance from him.

Finally, after six months in which this apparition of his beloved visited him every day, he heard her voice. She spoke with him about the joys of heaven, about the happiness of the loving ones in that blessed abode, and filled his heart with such desires for the other side that, if he had not feared sinning, he would have shortened his life himself. He conversed with her over this topic, but she advised him against such a step because it would part them from each other for a long time. Thus he obtained composure by and by, and lived with his supernatural beloved as happily as some are unable to do with those in the here and now.

His behaviour was noticed by the crew and the officers feared for his mind. The captain said, "Perhaps ambition plagues him; I have already experienced examples of such. I will raise him to sergeant, that will make him sensible again." — This decision was immediately shared with Wipner, along with the instructions for his new post; but he declined this honour absolutely. "I cannot be strict," he said, "and it would incur some responsibility; now I will trust in the sense of my superiors and action their commands to the best of my abilities." The captain wanted later on to bring him under the category of his servants on account of his reliability. Wipner did not reject this straightaway, but made the remark that he feared losing the favour of his master with it because he lived several hours of the day only for his feelings, whereas all outer contacts were repugnant to him. In his current circumstances, however, he could for the period of service follow himself the stirrings of his heart.

The captain desisted from his desires, but gave an order to observe him precisely in order to get behind the cause of his strange behaviour. Someone put the effort into winning his trust, and enticed from him a part of his secret. "He is a visionary," the informant said to the captain, "he converses daily with spirits for several hours." The latter smiled and suggested that if it were nothing more, then you could let him have his whims.

The Image of the Beloved

The spirit of his beloved told him in advance of everything that concerned him, and he was a few times, if not the saviour, a great benefactor of the entire crew because he warned them of future calamity.

One evening he desired to speak to the helmsman and told him, "Tomorrow we will have a storm; if you are not careful, we will all perish." The helmsman felt somewhat affronted by the admonition for caution, but restricted himself to a few questions.

Helmsman: When will the storm come?

Wipner: In the second hour after midday.

Helmsman: From which direction?

Wipner: From the south. If you let yourself get led astray by false wind gusts from the west, we are lost; in the direction to the south nothing can happen to us.

Helmsman: Who told you that?

Wipner: That is of no account; enough, I know it and consider it my duty to report it.

Helmsman: I will take my measures. God bless!

The helmsman, on account of the strangeness, made the captain aware of this conversation. The latter, although he did not believe in such prophesies, gave the order to make everything fast because Wipner's behaviour was quite apt for unusual things.

The next day, about one o'clock in the afternoon, the heavens began to move. At two o'clock the storm broke powerfully so that you did not know straightaway from which part of the heavens it was coming. The oscillations of the air flew about, the sea made a circling movement, but at once the the most emphatic southerly was signalled, and had the helmsman not previously given the ship the direction, he would, by his own admission, have ended in the greatest embarrassment, but the storm luckily passed over, and the captain declared that they had the sailor Wipner to thank for much that day, if not for the saving of the ship.

One day he spoke to his sergeant, "Report to the captain that tomorrow morning there will be an alarm on the ship. Three warships are coming to attack us, but courage and cleverness can rescue us. The first ship, if we offer it no resistance, but make believe our crew is too small and incapable of fighting will board; by that we win that ship, take the crew out of the battle and make the other two indecisive in their attack. They will certainly sail at us, but our cannons will damage one of those ships so much that the third will lose courage over it, take flight, and leave the other two as good booty for us. Tell the captain I said it and so it will happen."

"He seems to be a miracle man, Wipner," the captain said at this report. "If that occurs, then I do not know anymore what I should think about him; but we will take our measures; caution is better than remorse."

It happened as Wipner said. At ten o'clock of the second day, there appeared three ships with Portuguese flags, Portugal claiming sole rule in those parts and declaring any vessel of another nation as a good prize. The captain had the greatest part of his crew go armed into the hold, and kept on the foredeck only the weak and old. Since no sign of resistance was made, the first ship sailed quickly to the Dutchman, boarded and took the few people on the foredeck captive. But now the armed group broke forth and conquered in a few minutes the enemy ship and its crew. The others saw the turn in the battle and were suspicious; but finally they approached with full charges; but the cannons of the Dutchman struck so well that one ship sprung a leak and had to abandon the attack; the other took flight and left to the victors the two well-manned and well-provisioned warships.

After this victory the captain assembled the crew, and spoke in the following way to them, "It would be unfair if I or one of us ascribed to ourselves the honour for this day; it belongs alone to our good comrade Wipner. He announced the attack two days in advance and gave the plan of defence as well. To him we give thanks for our victory today over an enemy more than two times stronger. I will report his service to the government so that they will reward his time appropriately. But in order to immediately show him the recognition of our thanks, I am appointing him our ship's master by the power of my command; in this post he is independent, limited merely to the procurement of our needs, and can give free rein to his urge to be useful to us." Everybody called out in unison, "Long live the captain! Long live Wipner, our ship's master!"

The Image of the Beloved

It would be going too far to describe all his experiences and premonitions here, enough to say he was the ship's greatest benefactor and it had him to thank in the main for the successful battles and discoveries which it made on its journey. After fifteen years absence it landed again on the shores of the fatherland. Wipner took his leave to spend his days in the place of his birth. With wistful heart he entered the locale of his childhood where he had left his beloved and had no hope of seeing her again. He entered his father's house. Both parents were still alive and could not conceive for a long time how it was possible to see their son again whom they had lamented as dead. When the first outpourings of hearts was over, the mother said, "Oh, Else will rejoice when she learns of your arrival. She has turned away every suitor and declared she would not offer her hand to any other."

The son looked at his mother full of astonishment and said, "Else is dead and is waiting on the other side for me, that I know well." — "No," his mother answered, "Else lives! I will send straightaway and let her know of your arrival." — "One moment;" Wipner said. "How could that be? Else's spirit accompanied me the last twelve years and gave me daily news of the blessings of love in the other life! How could that be possible if she still lived?" — "It is so," the father remarked now; "she lives and has remained nice, cared for her parents, and buried them with a child's love. She visited us often in order to help us like a daughter and to console us when age and the sorrow over you falls hard on us."

Wipner could not get his head right for a long time. Finally he made the decision to see her beforehand unnoticed, before he spoke with her. Opportunity was soon found for it, and with wistfulness he noticed the difference between the original and his spiritual beloved. The former had become about fifteen years older, the latter though had entirely the looks of her first blossoming where all the magic of youth united in the cheeks in order to draw the heart of the beloved ever more firmly to itself. He returned sadly to his parents and said, "I do not know what I should do; the beautiful image which revealed itself to me daily leaves the natural Else so far behind that I fear that if I offered her my hand I would not meet her with such love as her virtue deserves. I am undergoing a difficult test and do not know how I shall pass it."

In the evening he was sitting wistfully alone and thinking about his fate when the spiritual beloved appeared to him as before. He feasted on her lovely sight, his heart dissolved into delight, and he made the decision to remain true to her; then he heard the words, "Do not hesitate to fulfill your promise!" He wanted to speak, but the apparition had vanished. "What should I do?", he asked himself. "Fulfill the promise!", his inner being gave the answer. "Right, I will obey," he now said out loud; "what she says is infallible, I must not resist." He went the next day to Else, after he had spoken properly with her, he offered her his hand, married her, and hoped for future enlightenment over the miraculous apparition.

The story is quite well-known. After three years a stranger came and had Wipner tell him about it. After that man had heard everything, he said, "The Else who appeared to you is her image arisen in your heart and was appearing to you as an impression of your love. Remain true to this, for it is a witness to your refound inner life; follow it as before and it will serve you and your wife as protection from mishap and prepare eternal bliss in that life."

***

The Doppelganger

A certain noble von Härdteck, captain in the 6th Line Regiment at P...rch, had a strange experience. — His parents put him in the Cadets' Institute, though he had not shown any special affinity for the military caste. He fitted very well into his new career though, was industrious, learnt the service alongside other subjects in the most punctual way, and when he appeared on parade, he was especially considered for the expediting of his future advancement. Härdteck advanced soon to captain, and only now did he get time to think about the nature of his caste. "It is difficult," he said once to himself when he was walking about deep in thought, "to connect the actual human with the soldier, as the latter, under too strict a form, very easily loses himself in this and considers it to be his nature. But even then, when the forms are strict, the heart must be yielding and humane, if you shall not strive against the first aim of human nature, the law of humanity."

He had spent three years as captain amidst such considerations and with the most punctual fulfillment of duties, then he often felt a strange stirring in his inner being and in his head. "What is it?", he thought; "shall my brooding have damaged my health, or confused my mind?" He paid close attention to himself, but found nothing which disturbed him in his actions.

One evening he found himself alone in his room, when it seemed to him as if something were stirring at his side, he looked over, but that which he intended to see turned back with his turn. He looked again straight ahead and saw that a figure stood to his right which with some effort, in that he turned only his eyes to the side, but not his head, he recognised as his image. He could not fend off an involuntary shudder and left the room in order to be rid of this company.

Outside the house he indeed did not see the figure anymore, but it was always as though he sensed it. "What shall become of it?", he thought, "I am no Sunday's child who sees spirits."

The next day, at the same hour, the experience recurred; but this time much clearer than the day before. When he sat down, it sat next to him, when he walked up and down in the room, it accompanied him, and when he stood still, it also remained standing.

"That is not an illusion!", he cried out, "for I am clearly conscious of all my other impressions. What shall I do? Who to confide in? — They will not believe me, will even mock me. I must remain silent and cannot do anything, as unusual as the matter also is, but face it with a manly courage."

Härdteck had already been engaged to Miss von Blum for a long time, but could not obtain permission to marry in the meantime. A third petition from him already lay with the War Ministry, to which the answer could follow at any moment. After three days, the colonel came up to him at the changing of the guard and congratulated him on his imminent wedding. "The approval of the King," he said, "has arrived, in an hour at most you will receive the copy and with it all obstacles will be removed."

In his current state this news did not cause him any such joy as he would have earlier felt; as he was duty-bound to inform his bride of his strange condition, and he was doubtful as to how she would take it. "Up to now," he thought, "human affairs have delayed my happiness, now heaven perhaps gets in my way, or at least a spiritual being hinders me." With apprehension, he resolved to go to his fiancée. What he suspected happened; she was horrified at the tale of his spiritual company, asked for a delay to consider and to speak with her parents. Härdteck achingly took his leave from her and said, "My heart loves sincerely, and I would, if you were in my position, not need to consider. But I will not complain, instead leave me the hope that your heart will conquer the fear."

He spent two days in fearful uncertainty, on the third he received a letter from the father of his beloved in which that man explained that under the prevailing circumstances the intended wedding could not take place. He regretted having to give a man of honour such an answer, only the love for his daughter made it necessary; meanwhile he counted on the uprightness of the captain and hoped the friendly stance which had been in place up to then between them would not be interrupted by the dissolution of the above mentioned relationship.

Härdteck read this letter with silent resignation, and said finally, "I am not destined to be happy, and I must bear this loss as difficult as it may also be for me!"

The permission of the king, as well as the imminent marriage between him and the young lady was generally well-known, it therefore struck everyone when the affair, in the moment when it was supposed to come to its conclusion, fell apart. The officers of the regiment saw in it an affront to their comrade and desired satisfaction from the father of the bride. The colonel himself had the captain brought to him in order to make him explain the precise situation. Härdteck explained that he alone was at fault for the break-up, because things had taken place which only related to him, but were not to be revealed." The colonel pressed him to give just a single reason in order to calm the officer corps. After resisting for a long time, the captain finally revealed to him that for some time a spirit had been walking next to him and never left him. Miss von Blum, whom he had informed about this unusual situation, could not master her fear and thus put an end to the engagement.

The colonel looked at him, taken aback. "What spirit!", he said, "That is a fancy which you have been tending to in your loneliness, and will vanish by itself once you have a wife. Your intended is a fool whose head must be set right." Härdteck defended her and asked the colonel not to undertake anything which could aggrieve or compromise her. The colonel finally agreed, but added, "Your condition must not remain thus! Ask the doctor for advice, perhaps he knows a means for banishing such unbidden company."

The captain, although he had the conviction that medical help would bear no fruit here, nonetheless followed the colonel's advice and spent half a year with useless cures. But then he dispensed with all outer means and declared that he considered his condition to be a fate which he must bear for as long as until it left him by itself. The colonel responded, "Well! Then do what you think is good for you; I want though to make one more attempt off my own bat. — When I still lived in the capital," he continued, "I got to know in a club a man who without any boastfulness and in complete seriousness made it known of himself that he had obtained the gift of knowing everything; he therefore invited everyone to turn to him in unusual affairs where human cleverness did not suffice anymore, in order to receive advice or help from him. To this man I will write, and if his words were not mere empty phrases, then he can perhaps give us information."

He wrote the letter that same day. In short time the following answer arrived, "The condition of your friend, which you conveyed to me, is of a peculiar sort; it stems from an all-too-great conscientiousness in that the captain doubts whether the better human nature lets itself be connected with the caste of soldiers. Through this struggle two beings have formed in him, a soldier and a normal human being; these two would like to unite with one another, but the indecisiveness of the possessor hinders them in it. Give my regards to your friend and tell him he should become friendlier with his spiritual companion, and strive to become one with it so that it passes into him and makes him into a complete man; then he will see that true human dignity excludes no caste and is bound to no clothes, but rather makes an appearance where the inner life releases itself from the outer, and stipulates for it the laws of thinking and acting.

If your friend takes to heart the contents of this letter and brings it into practice, then it will be good to give me from time to time news of the results so that I can put him right again in case he goes astray."

This letter made a great impression on the captain, and he cried out in astonishment, "He speaks of an inner life! Is the apparition which reveals itself to me surely the beginnings of that? I will follow this prescription and see what comes of it."

Härdteck kept his promise. The image which had been walking alongside him for a long time finally changed position and stepped in front of him, turned in circles with the circling of his thoughts, and began by and by to think and to speak in him.

"Humans are miraculous creatures," he said now to himself, "of spiritual and divine nature when they awake their inner lives, but dead without that, as much as they also take up learned theories into themselves. I acknowledge it, now I am on the path to the truth and my first duty is to thank my friend and the teacher obtained through him."

***

Ruppert's Family

Ruppert was district court judge in the provincial town of E...l. — He possessed alongside his income a respectable means and lived therefore in relationship to his colleagues on quite a good footing. In the first years of his residence there he had married the daughter of an official and she bore him three healthy children; with the confinement for a fourth, however, which was stillborn, her state of health was so disrupted that there was concern for her life. She could never entirely recover from this period anymore; the slightest heat and emotion seized her nerves and she often fell into a sort of fever which lasted several days. To her misfortune a malignant illness broke out which carried off her two youngest children, of which one numbered four years, the other five.

This blow hit both parents hard. The mother could not leave her bed for over quarter of a year and several times it was thought her end was nigh. In the end she recovered slowly, could by and by take part in the household again, and now directed her entire care and love to her still only seven years old daughter, Caroline.

She neglected nothing in her education, gave her instruction herself in the French language, found her according to her father's wishes a music teacher who visited her every day and discovered in her first-rate talents. Caroline made such progress that in her twelfth year, next to thorough knowledge of practical and elementary subjects, she could read, speak, and write French, and was considered to be a little virtuoso on the piano.

The father, delighted over such an education, could not resist the wish to live with his daughter in the capital in order to create for her in the circles there that candidness and lightness of behaviour which remained foreign to her in her present circumstances. In order to achieve this goal, he turned to a few of his influential acquaintances. Since by virtue of his knowledge and his reputation he belonged amongst the most honourable men of the land, his wish was taken into account and before half a year had flown by, he arrived in the capital as the chief justice.

Now a new life was beginning for the family. Raised in the capital, Ruppert felt as though placed in his original element and abandoned himself to all the impressions of public amusements which were going on at the time. Caroline thought she was only now beginning to live and achieved in a short time such a skill in genteel manners that nobody saw in her the provincial townswomen so easily. Of course her skillfulness on the piano contributed a lot to providing her so soon with the appropriate mettle; for wherever she appeared she was welcomed and admired. In this way five years passed as if in flight, five years in which her figure developed to a not so common beauty and drew suitors from all sides.

The son of the president, von Breithof, whose father was of bourgeois origins, but had been decorated with several orders and stood in great esteem, competed for some time very seriously for her favour. He had indeed already previously been engaged to the daughter of a certain counsellor, Hummer, but the qualities of his new beloved exceeded hers so much that he felt forced to use all possible pretexts to take back his word and offer heart and hand to Caroline.

The mother, who expected the revival of her health by the skilled doctors of the capital, saw herself betrayed in this hope though, not feeling happy in her new way of life. She often looked wistfully at her daughter when she bathed in the adulation of the world and her better self was subjected to the poison of envy. For the most part she was restricted to her sick room and could not accompany her daughter to the glittering parties where she was led by her father. "I see my child", she often sighed, "perishing before my eyes and cannot offer her a hand at all to save her." She indeed did not lack for admonitions, only the maternal voice was too weak against the tumult of the world and against the claims of the heart; Caroline swung ever higher in the admiration of society and with each new homage her desire for accolades grew.

Ruppert felt endlessly happy in these circumstances. When his wife dared to reveal to him her concerns with respect to their daughter, he declared them to be just fancies, the anxious fear of an ill disposition and thought only of providing for Caroline, his heart's favourite, the opportunity for new triumphs. For this reason, the solicitations of the young gentleman, von Breithof, were also welcome for him; he saw himself and his daughter already in advance in the higher circles, and delighted in the thoughts of seeing her just as honoured and admired there.

The mother finally became aware of this project of alliance. To start with she made no expression against it; but when she learned that Breithof had given up his previous engagement because of her daughter, she was quickly decided, "Breithof can never become yours," she said to her; "you must not be the object of envy and hate of another. The tears of the unfortunate woman who sees her happiness betrayed by you should not burden your heart. I beg you thus, yes, I command you to separate from your suitor with good manners and to dissolve an alliance which would inevitably make you unhappy."

Caroline heard this command with shock, for an alliance with Mr von Breithof flattered her vanity for which she had already made many sacrifices; her heart was also in play with it, for the emotions of love were shackling her stronger than she had ever suspected and so she felt at this moment extremely unhappy. The mother noticed the struggle of her soul and presented to her the consequences of such an alliance. Caroline cried and promised to obey, whereas without saying she hoped on the input of her father. The position of the thing remained accordingly with the parents, only she took care to keep the continuation of the relationship secret from her mother.

But this condition could not last long; Caroline's feelings themselves rebelled sometimes when she thought of her falseness towards her mother. Often she wanted to speak about it, but she lacked the courage; finally her mother learnt of the deceit, and lamented bitterly over the disobedience of her daughter. "I am a burden to you," she said to her and the father, "but heaven will soon free you of me, then you will see how much you have done wrong by me and how well-founded my warnings were."

The daughter's heart hardened still more; she could not respond to her mother with a word of consolation. But the father said, "The ill should not busy themselves with themselves anymore, but with others." The poor woman felt extremely unhappy and abandoned by such behaviour. "Lovelessness!", she sighed, "is the most terrible thing in a family, and this, I feel, is sending me to my grave."

She had spoken the truth. Her nervous attacks repeated with doubled ferocity and after twelve days the doctor declared her case to be hopeless. This sentence at once brought peace to the house. Caroline called herself a murderess, and did not move day and night from the ill woman's bed. Ruppert was also deeply shaken. "Wretched pride!", he said to himself, "You spurned humanity and then left us disconsolate in unhappiness." He undertook himself along with Caroline the care of the ill woman, but all their efforts remained fruitless; on the fifteenth day a nervous attack hit her and they watched any moment for her dissolution.

When she felt the end approaching, she stretched her hands out to her family, and said, "Forgive me, I forgive everything. You have no guilt in my death! If the dispute which arose between us brought it about, then it was a fate to which I was subject. I am calm and part from you with intimate love and will also think of you still in the grave. Do not forget me either, so that I live on in your memory. I desire no promises over anything, I only ask for one thing: do not rush so that late remorse does not incur for you reproaches of imprudence. Your happiness was my wish in life and also remains so in death; with this affirmation I will step before my judge in a few minutes."

She had spoken the last words in a barely audible way as she passed away to never again awake.

We will pass over the funeral, the pain of the daughter, as well as the sorrow of the father, and limit ourselves merely to the further life story of those left behind. Caroline reproached herself for having listened so little to the admonition of her mother, and resolved in future to not obey the demands of the world so blindly anymore. For this reason she became stricter towards the beloved and soon had opportunity to convince herself that his feelings had not been of as serious a nature as to last for their entire life. A rich rival captivated him and he repeated the same behaviour which he had applied to his previous fiancée. This pained her deeply, and from that time on she dedicated all her contemplation to the memory of her late mother. The falsehood of Mr von Breithof irritated the father so much that he cursed the moment in which he yearned for the capital. A different spirit came into his house, which made it the residence of silence, of sadness, and of displeasure. All his friends distanced themselves from him, and so he lived with Caroline in the populous city so withdrawn that you soon did not hear his name anymore in the circles of society.

A year passed, then Caroline's behaviour showed a conspicuous change. She became timid and shy, so that she hid from humanity and abandoned herself to a brooding which made her insensitive to all outer impressions. When her father pressed on her to reveal the cause of her behaviour, she said, "I do not know what is going on with me; often I am as if paralysed and then again so agitated that I am startled by the slightest little thing. In my inner being it undulates like the tides, and at night I hear without sleeping a clattering and voices around me which penetrate my nerves shaking and put me in a state as if I were lying in the most violent fever."

The father became scared at this talk. He asked the doctor for advice. The latter considered it to begin with to be somnambulism, but soon he noticed that here an entirely different mainspring lay at the base of it. He prescribed everything which he thought appropriate in the present case, but in vain. The agitated state remained, and the nocturnal episodes seemed to increase.

Now her state of health changed in a wondrous way; what she previously only felt and heard now appeared visibly before her eyes. The first attack of this sort happened on 4th April. She was sitting in her room towards evening as it began to get dark and was thinking full of emotion of the quick death of her mother and of the destruction of her life's happiness; then at once a racket arose in the room as if the walls were creaking, and table and chairs were moved from their positions. She started, looked about herself, and then saw a man of stocky stature, tanned face, and wild gestures rise opposite her and look at her with flashing eyes. She wanted to flee, but could not move from her spot for fright. Now the man spoke, "Why do you disturb me? Let the dead rest and live happily with the living." She wanted to answer, but was incapable of uttering a word and resigned herself to her fate in the firm conviction that this was her last moment. Finally the figure vanished as a thick cloud placed itself before him. Caroline recovered by and by from her fright, and rang for a light; when that appeared she looked about the entire room for the cause of the racket and the apparition, but could not discover the slightest trace anywhere.

The same man appeared amidst a similar racket on the next and following days again, and she could only free herself of him if she kept the piece of mind to ring for a candle. Embittered over it, he stepped quickly in front of her once and said, "Do not disturb me or you shall atone for it! From now on you must lend me your mouth, and I will tell the people stories they will be astonished about." When he said this, a horror penetrated her entire being and it was to her as if he had now taken complete possession of her. As soon as it got dark, someone brought a candle, and her consciousness was recovered again.

On the next day her father was with her. She told him what had happened. At once the floor creaked, audible only to her. She started and said, "He is coming now." The father grasped her hand and replied, "Be calm, I am with you." — "You are the right one too," it sounded from Caroline's mouth with a rough voice. "Child!", the surprised father cried out, "think and don't play jokes with me." — "Jokes! With you?", was the answer, "Who could do that? You are too stupid."

Ruppert looked stiffly at his daughter, and barely emitted the following words, "Is it you, Caroline, who is speaking here, then fear sin! If it is a different power which reigns in you, I do not know anything except that God is afflicting me terribly."

The voice spoke some more to the father and daughter; after an hour it fell silent, and Caroline had to go to bed because she felt so weak.

She had from this time on lost all courage, and a reliable person was taken on as a servant for her and to remain with her day and night.

Summer had arrived. Ruppert, on the advice of the doctor, travelled with his daughter to a spa town in order to distract her with strengthening cures as well as unfamiliar society and to banish the spirit; but it all remained without success.

On the 5th of August, when they were already home again, a new circumstance arose and they did not know whether it would lead to an improvement or a worsening of the malady. Caroline was with her companion in a garden on the outskirts of the city and said all at once to her companion, "Dear! What is happening with me? I see the stars in the bright of day." Her companion started, she was afraid of an attack of the spirit-seeing state, and made the suggestion of returning home. They left the garden together; but Caroline was seeing the stars on the way home and even in her room through the ceiling.

"What's happening with me?", she said sighing. "Why these apparitions when they to not lead to anything good? Oh! I see daily all the more that I am to blame for my mother. Why did I not stay true to her teaching? Why did I let myself be blinded by the vanity of the world?" — "Silent!", the voice of the spirit suddenly cried out from her, "or I will not give you any rest anymore. The stars that you see are flickerings of your brain; do not trust in them or you'll tremble!"

Caroline barely dared to speak any further, indeed, she was afraid of her own thoughts, for often at the slightest idea the spirit in her was awoken and burst out into loud imprecations. But the stars did not leave her anymore and she looked constantly to their shimmer in order to obtain refreshment from them. Once, when their brilliance was especially bright, a sort of cloud formed around one of them; the star transformed into eyes and finally into a quite lovely face which seemed to wave comfort and hope to her, she spread her arms out towards it, but in that same moment it vanished.

She wanted to express her joy over this apparition out loud, only the coarse spirit suddenly spoke again from her and reproached her bitterly. Caroline had accustomed herself through the course of time to fear this monster less and was also no longer becoming as weakened by its effect. Since the appearance of the stars and that lovely face, she won yet more courage and was resolved not to obey that monster so unconditionally anymore in future, but rather to act according to her own conviction and to trust entirely in the lovely image.

The evil spirit ranted violently at this decision. A racket arose as if the house wanted to collapse, but Caroline said, "I am accustomed to your episodes and will not be dissuaded anymore." He took over her mouth again at this talk, and emitted the most violent imprecations.

On the morning of 7th September Caroline again saw the lovely image emerge from a cloud. She did not turn her sight from it and tensed her ear in order to hear a sound from it; finally she thought she heard the following words, "Pay attention, I am entering you!" At once she felt an intimate stirring in her heart; she became so happy that she poured out tears of the most intimate thanks. The lovely spirit now took command of her mouth too, and spoke with soft, pleasant voice words of comfort and elevation. "Preserve me in yourself," it sounded from Caroline's mouth, "and do not let me be driven out again by that evil spirit who sought to lead you into the abyss." Hardly had she spoken this than that other one stirred, and the heart and mouth of the poor ill girl seemed to be the battle ground on which both spirits had established themselves in her and seemed to be waging war. She felt this and finally said in complete resignation, "As God wills it, I trust in him and will never abandon him anymore."

Ruppert, who had exhausted all means for helping her, did not torment her any longer with new types of cures; he did indeed do whatever was in his power for her amusement and recovery, but abandoned her undisturbed to her unhappy state. "It is a stroke of fate from God," he said, "and as such we must bear it patiently until he himself helps." He allowed upright and familiar people to visit his daughter because he had noticed that a calm company worked beneficially on her, and even when the spirits held conversations through Caroline's mouth, such visits suffered no interruption anymore because the matter through exaggerated caution could not get into the minds of the public.

One evening the commissioner Düprecht along with wife and daughter was with her. He had long since wanted to convince himself with his own eyes of the truth of the spirit possession of which so much was told. Since he belonged to those acquaintances previously well-known in the house, he conversed with Caroline in the most uninhibited way about her state of health and suggested that one should direct the spirits to where they belong, namely in the spirit world. Hardly had he spoken this than her face darkened, her eyes drew inwards, and the defiant spirit made his voice audible through her mouth.

Spirit: What are you saying, silly, irrational commissioner!
Düprecht: Be a bit more polite, if I may ask.
Spirit: Polite with you, who is my vassal?
Düprecht: Oh no! It is yet a good while until then!
Spirit: As you think — I know better.
Düprecht: See though! The spirit will not once get involved in definitions, so certain is he of his matter.
Spirit: You are a vassal, I say, and indeed so much so that you do not even feel your condition anymore. My comrade reigns in you and resides there so securely that he does not consider it worth the effort to make you aware of his existence.
Düprecht: Now I know, however, for you have told me.
Spirit: Yes certainly, you know it now, but you do not feel it, and what is all knowledge without this? Hahaha! Just be calm, after your death you will get to know us, then we will chevy you.

The commissioner turned pale at these words. He thought, if the evil spirit talks thus, just what will the good spirit say about me. The desire to ask had worn off from him.

"Cannot the good spirit also be heard?", the commissioner's daughter now asked. The above answered, "As long as the company of our rabble is present, he must not approach." The commissioner's wife started at this answer and called to her daughter to hold off from all further questions.

A trusted friend of Caroline's mother came one afternoon to visit. She had not returned to the house since the death of the mother because the memory was too painful to her. But now she had been brought here by the honest interest in convincing herself of the state of the daughter and, if she were capable of it, to offer her comfort and support. When Caroline saw her, tears appeared in her eyes, and she addressed the visitor with the following words, "Oh, dear friend of my mother! Do you come to see the unfortunate one left behind? If you can be for me what you were for my mother, perhaps I could again be delivered from my affliction! But for the children of the world to which I belong no friendship blooms; they are alone in unhappiness and abandoned."

The visitor talked encouragingly to the ill girl and gave her the assurance that she was attached to her with the same love as for the mother. She asked Caroline to confide in her if any secret sorrow weighed on her heart and to think she was transferring herself to a second mother. Caroline cried heavily at these words, then she dried her face and was wanting to speak, when her eyes turned inwards and the good spirit began speaking with lovely voice through her mouth, "Help her to fasten me in her." Caroline moved now violently and before she could get a hold of herself, the command resounded from her with coarse tones, "Away, and leave me in peace!"

The woman was horrified. When Caroline had recovered again, she said casually, "You see under what circumstances I live. I have to rely on unity, people are frightened of me in my condition and see in me a being which does not belong in their vicinity anymore. Oh! If only I lay with my mother in the grave." — "Calm down," the woman replied; "the sight of your condition surprised me, but did not deter me. You can bank on me, I will not abandon you, and I will visit you daily whatever might happen with you."

She remained with her the entire afternoon and a part of the evening. She had a few more opportunities to hear the utterances of both spirits. The good spirit seemed to think a lot of her, but to the evil one she was not welcome; only she paid no attention to it. While she affirmed Caroline of the most sincere sympathy, she promised to write to a relative for her sake, a mining inspector, who had helped often before in such cases. She kept her word and sent her letter directly the next day. The answer followed that the recipient of the letter, as soon as his business permitted him, would come to the capital and examine the state of the ill woman. According to the present information, he had all hope for a complete turn-around for the suffering woman.

Apart from the quoted conversations, the spirit enacted yet more wantonness through the entire house. The doors were often all opened; pieces of clothing were found in the garden, exchanged for garden tools in the wardrobes.

Once when Ruppert had been quickly called to the minister, his uniform could not be found; he made the visit without state dress and apologised over the confusion which reigned in his house. But hardly had he returned than he found the clothes in the uppermost room where the washing tended to be left to dry.

Another time, when the cook came into the kitchen, all the kitchen equipment was gone from there. She made a fuss in that she believed a thief had stolen them in the night. But later all the equipment was found in the wood shed artfully layered in a heap.

One morning as this cook was going into the cellar, she saw as she entered a bright blazing flame. She was violently shocked and hurried with screams of fear to the room of the master as if the spirit which she thought she had seen were following her. After she had recognised her mistake and recovered, she told of the cause of her shock. They went into the cellar and, in a place where it could not be dangerous, encountered a fire kept with split wood. A terrible tumult arose in the house; the servants declared they could not stay there anymore, and the owner terminated Ruppert's lease because he did not want to know that his property was in constant danger of fire. Great sadness followed this event. Ruppert said out loud, "Oh, if only for our mutual happiness death freed my daughter of an unfortunate existence!"

The friend mentioned above heard about this story, and went immediately to Caroline in order to hear the basis for it. She calmed the agitated minds and asked they wait just long enough for her cousin, the mining inspector, to arrive; the latter would certainly put everything in order again. Hence she wrote to him a second time to speed up his journey.

Both spirits had already been pressing for a long time to take over her. The gentle one often complained bitterly over the other that he stole her ease, used it to rob her of her faith, and now prevented her entry to blessedness. During his lifetime that one had been an usurer, had assembled many treasures, and buried them in the cellar of the house in order to now find them; as long as these precious things were not raised, she could not be freed from his persecution. The wild spirit pressed for the distancing of his disagreeable companion; only if he was again sole master could he put aside the coarseness and arrive at true happiness. Caroline suffered the most from these struggles and found herself not uncommonly in the greatest embarrassment — for if she made a promise to the good spirit, then the other raged, but when she wanted to promise the latter help, the gentle one began such a lament that she did not compose herself at all because of all the tears which it poured through her eyes.

Caroline revealed to a few people the secret over the treasure in the cellar, and the house owner, of whom it was said that he loved money a lot, shall really have made an attempt, but did not find anything. The wild spirit, who knew everything that happened inside and outside the house, made at least very funny remarks about it, and several people in the house were supposed in fact to have found fresh earth.

Both spirits also had in addition the gift of prophesy. The evil one became irritated or rejoiced often already two or three days before an impending visit. The gentle one knew just as well to give name to the pious bases from which it expected refreshment through spiritual sayings. It meddled even in the affairs of the house and spoke of future events as others spoke of the news of the day. This of course had to raise the interest which was taken in this spirit being, and it by and by allowed people of all classes to report in order to receive advice over entangled affairs or undertakings.

Once an estate owner, an old acquaintance of Ruppert, came with his wife and daughter to visit, with the intention of receiving some information about a projected marriage for the latter. The evil spirit said, "Marry the boy, for the single state does not suit you." The gentle one responded, "Consult beforehand with heaven!" Caroline, however, said in her natural voice, "If you have the blessing of your parents, then follow the path of your heart." — With these three it happened that each received the answers to their question from a different voice. The coarse spirit conversed with the father, the gentle with the mother, but Caroline herself always gave the answer to what was asked to the daughter.

Finally the longed-for mining inspector, Mohrland, appeared. The spirits which usually knew about all the visits beforehand seemed to have suspected nothing about this one, and there was a conspicuous calm amongst them when he seized Caroline's hand and asked her about her state of health. She could inform him undisturbed about everything and the power of the spirits seemed to be broken in his proximity. Ruppert rejoiced over this and took new hope. But the mining inspector affirmed that evil sat deeper than he had thought, for the calm was in no way a weakness, but rather cunning in order to lead him astray. He took proper notes and asked in addition to the father for another witness to his sort of cure on whose honesty one could rely in the case his conduct should be interpreted badly.

Ruppert suggested his doctor who had stood the test as friend and honest participant in his fate; Mohrland was content with that and promised to make a start straightaway in the morning with the cure.

The doctor arrived. He and the father entered the mining inspector's room to become mutually acquainted and to discuss the plan. Mohrland greeted the doctor and said, "It pleases me to get to know a man of integrity. What we undertake is unusual, because the efficacy of human powers is too little known and is mostly directed erroneously. In order to handle spirits, you must get to know them yourself and be familiar with their nature. In the present case, the usual way is not capable of anything anymore, but instead the free spiritual power must step into the centre and separate the evil from the good. Therefore do not expect that I will conjure spirits or drive out devils; I have only come to reestablish a lost balance in a human nature which has lost itself through violent withdrawal and abnormal awakening of the inner life. Both the spirits which reveal themselves in the girl are not beings from outside her, she is them herself. Disorderly desires, suppressed passions, guilty conscience, and other monsters have developed in her, risen into figures which grow in her, and obtain dominance over all her thoughts, wishes, and actions. She herself has sunk into a struggle foreign to her, our task is to free her from the pressure and to recreate for her her natural ego.

The doctor responded, "External means have been exhausted, and if help is possible, then it can only follow according to your plan which has the psyche of the ill girl in eye, and I consider myself lucky to be permitted to be a witness to a method of treatment which sees the spiritual as a means to reestablish a shattered human nature."

But Ruppert said, "I rely on God that he will illuminate you in order to free my daughter of an evil which is more terrible than any illness because it touches the innermost powers of life, and shakes both body and soul."

They made their way to Caroline. They were with her for over quarter of an hour, and no trace of one of the spirits residing in her was revealed. Finally Mohrland began and said, "Now you wild kobold, why are you so silent in my vicinity? Answer me, I command it!" Caroline's eyes turned and the spirit strained to talk, but soon emitted the following words in a sneering tone, "Leave me in peace!" Mohrland now directed his speech to the gentle one in that he said, "You too seem to be hiding yourself? Why are you so in awe of me?" The answer sounded as lovely as the notes of a flute, "You may not know me in my heaven." — "You are right there," the mining inspector replied, "I do not entirely like your heaven, it is the creation of an over-affected, but not pious disposition." The spirit sighed, and Caroline sat with skewed eyes silently in their company.

"Caroline!", the mining inspector now cried out, "are you sleeping?" She stirred spasmodically. "Caroline!", he repeated, "awake and answer me." The spirits seemed to want to speak; he grasped a towel which lay near her, threw it over the girl's head, and held it fast under her chin while he said, "Be silent or I will throttle you! I want to hear her, not you. Caroline, answer me, I order you!" She made a movement with her hands to remove the towel. Mohrland drew it away, and Caroline looked at those around her as if she were awakening from a deep sleep. "Hello, my daughter!", the mining inspector said. "Have you got rid of your unclean company?"

Caroline: I feel free.
Mohrland: For how long?
Caroline: That I don't know.

Mohrland: Why should you not know it, since you are mistress of your house?

Caroline: I have lost my dominion.

Mohrland: You must reestablish it.

Caroline: I am too weak.

Mohrland: I will stand by you. Do you want to accept me as an ally?

Caroline: Very much.

Mohrland: Then hear my conditions. Study your enemy so that you can utilise his weakness and become the victor.

Caroline: How can I do that?

Mohrland: Do not admit that one of them dominates. Neither the one nor the other is good, for both are just outgrowths of your actual life. Seek yourself, then you have the leader whom you may obey without danger.

Caroline: I indeed comprehend what you mean, but I am not capable of showing up my opponents.

Mohrland: Then you must learn obedience.

Caroline: I am ready for it; what do I have to do?

Mohrland: Diligently say 'I'! Your ego is suppressed by other powers, free it of them, and then you will be healthy again.

Caroline: I would give heaven for that!

Mohrland: Just courage and trust! Follow my teaching and you will see that I, supported by your better nature, will soon establish calm in you. Tomorrow I will come again, show that you are an obedient daughter.

He offered her his hand, and left. Ruppert and the doctor followed him without saying a word. Caroline fell after this visit into an unusually sleepy state and slumbered almost the entire day. The next day the doctor arrived punctually at nine o'clock in order to again be present as a witness to the way of healing of Mohrland, and they proceeded with the father to the ill girl.

This time she was in an excited state. Her spiritual guests in-residence seemed to have united in order to therefore conduct a more secure resistance to their enemy. At the gentlest allusion to Caroline's state of health, the wild spirit answered with ferocity and threatened the mining inspector. Even the gentle spirit mixed into its melodic tones words of reluctance.

Mohrland called Caroline by name again like the day before. But when she wanted to speak, it was as if somebody was squeezing her throat. He touched her neck with his thumb, and she thus regained power to talk. Mohrland said, "Does Caroline not yet have the courage to obey me?"

Caroline: It would be different if I had the strength.

Mohrland: It lies within you.

Caroline: I have not found it and do not know how to seek it either.

Mohrland: The spirit of a human is simple. You have split yourself up and hence you are without the means to struggle. Collect your powers again in a basket, in the feeling of your ego which speaks in your heart and you are free.

With tense attentiveness, Caroline listened to him. Her chest rose with his talking. He placed his hand on her back, and continued, "You have distanced yourself from the altar of your life and proceeded to its cupola. The heart is the position where our nature obtains certainty and freedom, there you must again learn to feel and speak, otherwise there is no help for you. The head is the last instance of our activity; only when we have made experiences of friendship and love in our disposition may the head think about them. When we seek the results of our thinking before we have the experience, phantoms arise which plant themselves, germinate, grow, and finally envelop us entirely. Withdraw the activity of your senses from your head, sink your eyes, ears, smell, and taste down into your body, let the invisible, spiritual pores again obtain their natural course and not play outwards, then you will feel what power emerges from it, and how naturally we confess our freedom to ourselves and are capable of preserving it."

It seemed as if she not only heard every word of his, but immediately put them into action. She breathed a few times from the depths of her heart and, when he stopped talking, she responded, "You have touched the root of my illness and I feel today quite clearly that you can remove it. But it will cost effort ... hence stand by me!"

Mohrland took her hand and continued, "You are an obedient daughter and hence we will immediately make an attempt at strongly opposing your enemies. Your house is undermined, the foundations of it loose, hence we must stand firmly on our feet and take from the enemy the hope of knocking us over easily. Do you have the courage to appear strong?"

Caroline rose, stood herself in front of Mohrland, and said, "Here I stand." — "Well now," he continued, "now the spirits shall reveal themselves if they are capable." Everyone was tense, but Caroline stood calmly. "Have you become dumb?", Mohrland continued. Caroline's eyes began to turn, but he had barely noticed this when he called to her, "Stand firm!" At the same time he drew her arms down to her body and commanded her not to stretch the corners of her mouth upwards. It succeeded; for her eyes returned again and Caroline had in this way carried the first victory over her enemies.

Mohrland gave her praise over her conduct, and said, "Practise standing on steady feet and thinking in your heart 'I', then we will soon meet our goal."

He departed with his companions. The doctor could not show enough surprise over this process and demanded explanations of it; but Mohrland responded, "I think it will all become clear to you in the process of the treatment."

The next morning, as Mohrland came with his friends to the ill girl, she was quite calm. "How did you sleep?", was his address. "The night was quite good," she gave as her answer, "only I felt in my feet sometimes a strong burning feeling which did not let me sleep." — "Well," he said, "the roots of your proper life are spreading quickly, that is a good sign." He placed his hand on her back again and tempted the spirits out. Immediately Caroline's eyes turned inwards, the gentle spirit sighed and the coarse one made his reproaches audible. Mohrland asked sternly, "You evil outgrowth, how long will you yet reside in this body?"

Spirit: As long as it pleases me.

Mohrland: Well now, it will please you then to sink into yourself and rob yourself of all power, to serve instead of dominating. You are a subordinate power of Caroline's, how can you now be so foolish as to rage against yourself? If you corrupt her, then you will perish with her, but if she wins herself back, you both could unite with her as one and live on.

Spirit: Pah!

Mohrland: Choose! Either you do what I desire, or I will remove you from her the way you remove a sick limb from the body and throw it out into the waste. You are a corrupt limb of life and have therefore only two paths, either to become healthy or to be cut away.

The spirit let out a howling sound, and fell silent. "Dear daughter," Mohrland continued, "you have struggled above my expectation! Continue thus and soon all will be good. Listen now to my further instruction.

"I will leave you for four weeks; remain steadfast during this time. The spirits will often make attempts to win mastery over you again, hence be careful. Give your eyes humility! That is, turn your pupils downwards so that the brain is not blinded by their radiance. Place your right hand two inches under the stomach and pray to God for mercy. Mercy is your prayer. Give mercy, great God, to your girl! Think thus incessantly; without any gestures, without any movement of the mouth, merely speaking in your inner being, sticking hard to the soles of your feet, seeking from there out the seat in the heart, then we will see whether we will not in four weeks be singing songs of praise together."

Caroline immediately had a go at the above prayer and the pose. The coarse spirit wanted to stir. Mohrland threatened it, and said, "I command peace and announce that if the ghost stories in the house do not stop and Caroline does not get rest, then you must go to where the Bible sends you." — "Oh!", it sounded hollowly from the mouth of the ill girl, and the calm on her face and in her disposition was established.

Mohrland left the room with the others. Caroline practised her task, but was so overpowered by sleep that she needed to lie down on the sofa. The doctor had a lot on his heart today for which he wished an explanation and hence turned to Mohrland.

"Just allow me two questions before you leave. You seem with Caroline to be working merely on her limbs and pay no heed to her ability to think, to her mind. Should she not before everything else learn to think again properly?"

Mohrland: How can she do the latter as long as the life from which the tree of thoughts germinates and which gives it nourishment is in disorder?

Doctor: It sounds strange, but considered more closely, I must myself say it is the only true way. The plant without suitable earth cannot flourish; to the contrary, it perishes by and by. From where though does the power come to the spirits to effect such disorder in the house?

Mohrland: Through the person in whose possession they are. They force and drive her to actions which are often very difficult and strange, so that the common person comes to the conclusion that the hands of spirits have acted here, meanwhile the person controlled by them accomplished those acts.

Doctor: But what misled her to it?

Mohrland: Ask the sleepwalker why he wanders about and often visits the most dangerous places. The spirit forces them and gives them the adroitness necessary for it. It knows the time to lead its tool unnoticed, and it must obey its will without knowing it or being able to recall it. Believe me! All is in the inner being of the human, not external to it, and with the grisliest haunting, with the most diverse such phenomena, it is always only those who are capable of seeing them and hearing their clatter whose spirit powers are agitated and in a sort of dream or clairvoyant condition.

Doctor: If that were so, then humans would indeed only have to study alone in order to recognise phenomena of this sort and to arrive at the highest knowledge.

Mohrland: Do you believe then that another way is possible? Must you, in order to get to know a type of wood, dismember all the trees of its species? Certainly not, one suffices; but you investigate that one from the roots to the crown, from the bark to the innermost core; as a result you obtain the knowledge of the entire species. What you then do further consists only in the comparison of the one with the others, which is though impossible without a thorough understanding of an individual one, but presents no difficulty with the last ones.

Doctor: But knowledge of humanity is of a different sort to knowledge of plants?

Mohrland: Admittedly; in so far as the human is of a different sort; the knowledge, however, is only obtained in the above way. In every individual there are all the characteristics of the species; each is only a repetition of the other and hence we must necessarily limit ourselves to the investigation of that detail which is given to us. The human is not master of another, but rather only of himself; hence he can also only recognise the other in himself. The matter is as clear as two times two equals four. But if we do not see this truth to be as simple as it is, then that comes about because we have accustomed ourselves to look, instead of at us, only at others who then show us what they like and lead us, instead of to truth, to errors.

Doctor: I understand and see that you are right, indeed must be right if the investigation of human nature is possible at all.

Mohrland: It is possible; on that, instead of any proof, take my word for now. Now I must make preparations for my departure. I hand over my patient to you. Physical harm, tooth and earaches will occur; do not use any radical cures for them, but content yourself with using alleviating methods.

Mohrland departed the same day. Caroline was quite free of spirit haunting for the first few days. She practised the tasks which the mining inspector had prescribed for her, and felt the affect of them after fourteen days; her heart won more strength, she was more receptive to the outer life, but in her ears it began roaring and violent pains shuddered through her jaws as if fire were raging in them. Now the spirits also began to stir again, but despite the suffering she succeeded for the most part in withstanding their attacks. At night her sleep was interrupted by a pounding and noises only audible to her. Several times it drove her out of bed in order to undertake nocturnal wanderings. But the spirits had for the most part lost their caution, for now several house residents saw Caroline walking about and exercising the strangest escapades. If you made her explain herself the next day, she did not know the slightest about it. "Mohrland is right," the doctor said after several such items of proof, "and now I also believe that he possesses more knowledge in such cases than we do with our extensive systems, and that his doctrine of seeking everything in oneself is grounded in nature." The evil which the mining inspector had foreseen appeared most punctually with much force. The doctor followed his prescriptions, and when Mohrland returned again, he found him right then with Caroline prescribing her some palliatives against the aforementioned pains.

"I see," Mohrland said, "that my patient was diligent, otherwise the doctor would not be with her. What are the unbidden guests up to? Are they not yet defeated?" The doctor reported everything that had happened since. "Good," Mohrland responded, "soon we will be at our goal." He took Caroline by the hand and directed several questions to her which she answered with confidence and a clear mind. The voice of the gentle spirit had almost been completely lost and was uniting itself with Caroline's natural voice. The coarse spirit, however, did not want to set aside its ferocity, hence Mohrland threatened it and promised it a shameful end. "You are unworthy," he said, "of remaining in life, hence remove yourself from this house in which you are being arrogant and prepare yourself for your fate. From now on, all your sustenance will be taken away; you shall not command anymore any sound, any look, or any gesture, and if you then starving and thirsting cannot hold yourself anymore, then leave us in peace and fester in the night from which you arose." The spirit made every possible attempt to set itself against these orders, but the mining inspector looked his patient firmly in the eye, grasped both her hands, and breathed spiritual powers through all entrances into her.

"The throne is erected again," he said solemnly, "and all that remains is to fly to it. Dear daughter! Just a short moment of courage and you will see what a reward you will share. You have learnt to position yourself, now you must seek to defend yourself. The power lies in your hands to do so. From the fingertips pass the flames of life which nothing impure can withstand; seek in these the life, and where something stirs which wants to harm you, then use them as weapons. Continue to practise what I taught you to pray, and soon your better life will have obtained the victory."

Caroline listened attentively, and while he spoke she felt her hands and fingers coming to life. She immediately made a few attempts, but became so exhausted by it that she fell into a slumber in the presence of Mohrland and the doctor. The former said, "She puts men to shame — she has in a short time obtained a power which astonishes me. In a few weeks she will have come so far that she will not need me anymore, but instead can help herself and bring it to fruition."

It happened thus too. She indeed still had a few struggles to overcome, aches of all sorts burrowed into her flesh and into her bones, only she remained steadfast and said, "either live right or not at all!" Two months later, it was evening, she wished to be alone in order to abandon herself entirely to her inner activity when she felt suddenly so moved that she thought the floor was swaying under her. But she remained steadfast and thought, "it is perhaps the crisis; away with all that did not originally belong to me!" The struggle became more and more violent and finally it seemed to her as if something were releasing itself from her body and vanishing into the darkness. She felt at once so light that she thought she could rise into the air. "Mercy, you are eternally merciful!", she said, "I feel you have freed me from my evil." —

The next morning she was very weak though without being ill. "I seem so young," she said, "that I barely trust myself to stand on my feet." This condition lasted for eight days; finally she felt strong again, and for the first time she walked as a healthy person amongst her house companions.

Mohrland, who had meanwhile been away again for two months, drove up to the house. She noticed him already from the window before the carriage came around the corner, and hurried to the front door to receive him. He saw her and placed his hand on his chest to thank her. She likewise raised her hands to the heavens and said, "There is your reward, people cannot repay you." — "Dear daughter!", he said as he climbed down from the carriage, "the joy you give me cannot be described." — "I am your daughter," she answered, "for you have given me not only my life, but a new existence in God. I am free of all enemies and have the light of heaven in me."

Mohrland now stayed a few weeks with Ruppert in order to fortify Caroline for the future and to give her instruction in learning to recognise the inner life which she had obtained in its purest light. She listened and understood his words now, and if she was still in doubt over anything, she could usually obtain the explanation herself.

One morning, as she was abandoning herself to her spiritual contemplations, she noticed that most of the previous phantasms which she became aware of in such a state showed themselves only darkly or not at all. Among these phenomena, however, the image of her mother unveiled itself and incorporated the others into itself as it were. She lingered for a long time in this contemplation, and when Mohrland came with the doctor to visit, greeted her, and was made aware of these phenomena by her, he said, "Now we are at our goal! You have seen your "I" in its origin, in the image of your mother, now we may rejoice and praise the miracles of the creator."

The doctor, who had meanwhile been observing the entire course of the healing, said, "Are they miracles that I have seen, or is this condition so natural that anyone can obtain it and look again into their original ego?"

Mohrland offered him his hand and replied, "You have by your persistence and loyalty obtained a right to all revelations of this seeming puzzle; so listen. All religions, we know, begin in a primitive state which has been left and should be called on again. Christ must suffer, die on the cross, rise again, and obtain the kingdom of heaven. The Adamites were driven out of paradise and must with spiritual powers render harmless the flaming sword which defends it. The Egyptians have the dead seek the path of life from the labyrinth. Cerberus* denied the Greeks entry to Elysium. — If you consider this closely, you find with our patient almost all the struggles described above; but the image of Cerberus becomes especially clear to us through its wild spirit. Everywhere there are obstacles to the entrance into our actual life, and as long as we do not perceive all of these — be they of whatever sort, rough or gentle, kindly or vindictive, white or black — and do not struggle with them and vanquish them, we are in the labyrinth, still outside paradise, not in the kingdom of heaven, and have no hope of those blessings which are promised to the fighter and victor."

"Can I obtain the entrance to the better life as securely as happened with Caroline?", the doctor asked. "Why not?",

---

* [Tr.: Cerberus was a giant dog in Greek mythology which had many heads and guarded the entrance to Hades.]

Mohrland replied. "The powers for it are given, and it would be a shame for you, if you had to remain outside the house. Seek the entrance, and even if it plagues the old, twisted man a little, think that nobody, not even the sinner, comes through this earthly life without pains. Why shouldn't you withstand a few storms to obtain the certainty of it?!" The doctor grasped his hand and said, "I want to find the entrance or not live anymore. Be my support if I become hesitant and come to my help, like to that patient, with spiritual powers and instructions."

He kept his word and learnt to know himself. But Caroline recovered more from day to day, and developed a rare purity of soul — she was conscious of her talk and actions in such a way that she gave information to all who asked her for advice, and gave her father an old age such that he even in the last days of his life said, "My daughter has called me to the real existence and shown me thereby a happiness which is tied up with us and can neither disappoint us nor abandon us."

***

Continuation of the Oral Instruction

After six months, Silbert appeared at Fielding's with a demeanour which immediately revealed that his ego did not remain without impact and it had shaken the mind of the doubter violently. When the first greetings were over, he began, "I have undergone hard struggles; my body bristles against my diligence and my mind reproaches me for my mechanical obedience, but the will remains master! I have continued my exercises and have now won the conviction that much is to be obtained which is barred to the common man." Fielding inquired about every circumstance of his activity in particular, had every effect of it told to him, and then made him aware openly of his joy that he had justified his expectation. "You have acted like a man," he said; "this obliges me to guide you further. Hence listen — humans must see, hear, and feel themselves — not only outwardly, but also inwardly — to be created in the image of the spirit, which always agrees with the state of our soul. We perceive the first of these phenomena, as stated already previously, in dreaming, then also when awake, and finally in the most complete clarity of our powers of thinking. You have passed the tests of that in yourself, hence let us put the phenomena in order.

"The power of the ego has penetrated you so that you have arrived at the conviction your entire being is capable of the conception of the spirit. But since the ego pays tribute to so many forces, following today this, tomorrow that ability, we want to show it the path to where it will find its better self again, the pure human nature separated from all the circumstances of the world and raised to dominance.

"The primitive human is born to be a leader. What the world gives us is transient and weak. When the class rules over the human, when an ego which takes the world as given rules us, then we are in darkness, and fall victim, if we do not save ourselves, to death. The pure ego, however, when it triumphs over the others, subjugates death and opens for us the entrance to life; hence we want to get directly through to the human and learn both to feel it in us and to distinguish it in us. To this end, practise in future thinking the name "man" until the power of it grips you, destroys the false seeds completely, and puts you in the standpoint where only the stamp of humanity has value to you. — You have completed the first task, attempt now the second.

"With us it is harvest time, hence my hours are measured; but I advise you to stay a few days with me in order to see the diligence and joy of the country people when they bring their yield home. It leads our disposition closer to nature when we observe in what fullness it gives, and we forget, at least for moments, that humans also cast the spell on their products which leads to many a discontentedness."

Silbert stayed and watched the liveliness of the inhabitants of the district and practised his task in passing. It awoke in him entirely different sensations to the previous task. "I feel myself inside and outside," he said to Fielding, "when I carry out the new task." — "Just be brave," the latter said, "for you must possess yourself from within and from without."

One evening, when Fielding had finished with his business earlier than usual, they were sitting on a hill together; before them lay the glorious landscape in the most beautiful evening light. Silbert became spontaneously enraptured and cried out, "Nature is wonderfully beautiful, sublime beyond all expression and all description! Can then the spiritual eye see yet greater beauties?"

Fielding: The spirit sees everything in its own light.

Silbert: I do not understand that.

Fielding: From the spirit comes everything which is. In it are the rays of life, as well as all the forms and colours which delight our eyes. It is the embodiment of all beauty, and the outer world is only a weak copy of the lively brilliance in which it sees itself. The more we recognise the spirit, the more completely the creation also appears to us. Nature possesses no beauties for the spiritless.

Silbert: According to that, the wise man must have more pleasure than the unwise.

Fielding: Do you doubt it?

Continuation of the Oral Instruction

Silbert: No. But the matter seems ambiguous to me. Wisdom requires dispensing with all pleasure, and yet it shall preserve the receptivity for it?

Fielding: That is wordplay, borrowed from the unwise who in their barrenness do not want to tolerate any abundance. Who made the plan for the creation? The eternal wisdom. Who can understand this plan? The wise man. And by what can he understand it? If he penetrates into the nature of the creation, considers it in its beauty and inner perfection, and thereby arrives at the highest pleasure.

Silbert: If that is so, then the teaching of wisdom is also that of pleasure.

Fielding: Bliss is our goal! In it we find all the conditions for life fulfilled.

Silbert: This is also the speech of the egotist.

Fielding: By appearance. Someone who brings a position in human society which was long despised back to honour again by their merit, are they an egotist? No, truly not! They have only in themselves put to the test the worth of their stance. This is the human's paragon: each shall strive to produce in themselves the ideal of humanity, then they will have worked for themselves and humanity.

Silbert: You are right. For the first time, this insight becomes clear to me. We want to enlighten others while we ourselves are wandering in the dark. I feel what I am neglecting and will strive through knowledge of myself to pay the debt which humanity had demanded from me.

He rid himself for an indefinite period of all legal business and dedicated himself entirely to his new activity. In order to live more untroubled, he even distanced himself from the city, and rented an isolated farmstead where he saw nobody around himself all day, and could continue his exercises both at home and outdoors. It lasted a year until he was capable of accounting for the success of the second task. But finally the bark cracked and he felt the necessity to visit his friend again so that the seed would not be damaged by false action.

When he came to Feilding, he said, "Humans must find themselves, each to themselves, then humanity ennobles itself. I have recognised the outer hull of the human, lead me into the interior." The latter responded, "You have pronounced what you need, the inner being. Seek it yourself! So that it will be yours though with certainty and without any deception, think to yourself for a year: inner nature!"

Silbert thanked his friend, and went away again. "Inner nature!", he said to himself, "I want to get to know you. Inner nature! You shall be my password."

Again a year passed and he came to the conviction that the human floats without complete metamorphosis, without rebirth, aimlessly on an ocean where he can never succeed in coming to shore.

Since now all the images which reveal themselves to the human in dreaming as well as when awake were becoming quite clear to him, he read once more the stories in that book mentioned above, so as to explain the causes of their effects.

"The scholar," he wrote in his diary, "is an example of that confusion in which so many fall when they set themselves a goal without considering the peculiarity of their nature. This man enjoyed himself in his position, used all the powers of his spirit to lift it to the highest peak; but his natural ego was thereby suppressed. He wrote for the most part books of moral content, for children, over their education, over the improvement of humans in specifics and in general, he went to battle against the vices of his fellow men, and everybody considered him to be an apostle of his time, a star which will yet illuminate future offspring. But all his writings were the fruits of his diligence, his ability to compare and to speak concisely according to given forms, but did not arise from his innate power. The scholar alienated himself from the natural ego, and died in his living body. The latter, enervated and weakened, could not rise to the rebirth, so it fell into the arms of the coarsest animal nature and finally into those of death.

I was on this path, and can only thank a kind providence that I was saved by Fielding while there was still time.

A charming example of rebirth is given to us by the story of the sailor who found the inner life in the image of his beloved. The tale does not indeed mention it, but he certainly saw her first in dream, then she came to him while he was awake, became his companion, and led him finally victorious through the storms of the sea to the shores of home.

This is an example of those simple natures of the fifth stage who obtain themselves in faith and love. Blessed are they who wander such paths.

The captain of P...rch stands awe-inspiringly before me. Out of fear of injuring the laws of humanity, the image of his uncorrupted ego steps to his side and takes him, in this life already, up into himself.

Sublime power of humanity, help me and everyone so that we finally see you in our image and unite ourselves with you.

The story of Caroline Ruppert is of a chaotic sort; various feelings struggle in me. The sorrow over her mother and the fear of conscience finally awaken her better ego. The feeling of a nourished vanity paired with a touch of piety act privately against her, and would have certainly ruined her had that enlightened mining inspector not come to her rescue.

Wondrous powers of the spirit! Even in confusion still elevated above the usual cleverness and reason because you can raise the veil of the future — why are you so seldom sought? Why are we not instructed to distinguish in your area good from evil? I thank you, eternal goodness, that you took me into your school! I thank my friend and benefactor who guides me with so much patience from the turmoil."

He practised for two years awakening and delving into his inner being. After this time he went to Fielding, and said, "The human and his inner nature are alive, but I feel in this yet an innermost core, I would like to say, a prime cause of my existence. Help me to unveil this too."

Fielding replied, "You are right! In the uttermost inner being a core is found which is preferred; this is also possible for the *ego*. But to satisfy everyone and to raise them to the level which is fitting for their courage and diligence, name it 'King' and you will see what power emanates from it."

Silbert remained a few days with his friend, strengthened himself on his words, refreshed his heart in the unfeigned evidence of friendship, and went in a happy mood again to working on himself.

The aim of it soon became clear to him, and before a year had flown by, he was already with Fielding again. The latter welcomed him and said, "We know the tree from the bark to the innermost pith; but now it is necessary to examine it for its height and depth. Hence I invite you again to visit my friend who is more perfect than I am. It is precisely that Mohrland whom you know from the story of Caroline Ruppert." — "It is!", Silbert exclaimed, "then it would be wrong on my part to not comply with you in everything, since you have directed me up to now with such love and forbearance."

The next day, they started on their way. They met Mohrland in his room, surrounded by stones and grades of ore. When he caught sight of Fielding, he went up to him, offered him his hand, and said, "Eh, look! What an unexpected delight! Greetings, my brother! What brings you to me?" — Fielding answered, "A new friend has been found; you shall help me guide him on the path which is laid down for us by nature."

Mohrland now also offered his hand to Silbert, and looked at him from head to toe as he said, "A well-built young man, there nature must have its joy." Silbert meanwhile had opportunity to observe Mohrland and recalled having seen him already before. But anyone who had at the time said he would yet be schooled by this simple mining inspector, he would have called a liar. This and other things he thought to himself.

Mohrland continued, "Nature, my friend, goes its calm way, led by eternal laws; we must research these, then we will stroll on the right path because we are called to live in the knowledge of those laws. I know you have already begun, and it is with you only about staying brave. Conviction of immortality is your special aim — you have chosen a good task which indeed is certainly troublesome to fulfill though. But anyone who urges forwards undismayed must become certain of it. Enough for now! I must now make arrangements to serve my dear guests worthily. How long will the visit last? Though not so short as usual?" Fielding remarked, "If it is not onerous for you, we will stay for three days." Mohrland made them aware of his pleasure over this, and left them for a few moments to make the appropriate orders.

The day passed quickly amidst the usual conversations about the circumstances of human society, about the actions and doings of the day, and about the confusions to which people were subject everywhere. The next morning, Mohrland said, "Today I want to also show our new friend my professional activity. He has perhaps never seen a shaft and it will be not unimportant for him hence to try out just once how it is to live under the earth." They set out on their walk, and before quarter of an hour had passed, they found themselves at the opening of the mine.

***

The Shaft

"Now let us descend into the pit;" Mohrland said after he had prepared Silbert properly. Arriving below, he showed him all the passages and turns of the shaft, and led him finally into a sort of niche in which a table and four chairs were found, along with papers and books. "Here is my living room," Mohrland said, "here in the womb of the earth, in the grave as it were, I abandon myself to the contemplation of the other side and the here and now, and can often barely comprehend how the people up above might be so foolish to torment and torture themselves for the few days which they may spend there. Here, I then think, is our home, in the grave is the exit and the entry to life; from the earth it must sprout if something well-made shall occur; for through the entire realm of creation we have yet to see any solid plants made of air, nor any made of fire, nor any made of water. Everything good which stands out by its activity or specific outlines must come from the earth.

"I have spent a great part of my life above, only later was I allocated down here by the fate of my sphere of activity; but I must confess, only here was I in a position to penetrate all the fog which lies about the life of humans; here I obtained an equilibrium which was quite alien to me previously, and as a result a new life course began for me.

"From youth on I was inclined to get involved in theosophical investigations and learning to comprehend the doctrines of those wonderful scholars; but since their writings are always incomplete and everything is to be understood more figuratively than literally, I could not untie the knots. I knew their metallurgy by heart, their applications and relationships of magnetic and sympathetic powers for the life, and even for the spirit itself, was attracted always to new investigations, but the blindfold would not leave my eyes. Here, deep under the residences of humanity, here, as it were in the body of God, I won a new, practical view. I am Pluto, I thought, and deliver metals to the world above. 'Where do I find them?', I then asked myself. — Here they are was the answer. But from where this suitability, this brilliance, this light in all the metals and stones? Do the colours and rays of Olympus penetrate as far as orcus*? Does Jupiter's power also reside in Pluto, and can Jupiter himself not exist without Pluto and Neptune? Everywhere there is light, everywhere water and air, everywhere the metallic power. Heaven is in the earth, the earth in heaven; water and air, however, are the messengers to prepare, to work, and to purify all the powers and mixtures. 'Nature with all its heavens is just one!', I cried out in delight. Humans can also arrive at unity and thereby achieve in the individual the perfection of the whole.

Humans are alive, I continued in my meditations; in what relationship now does the life stand to the great whole? Humans have bodies, feelings, and thoughts. The body is the earth, the thoughts the light, and the feelings are the bearers between the two. The thoughts must, as Jupiter the earth, penetrate and fill the entire body; likewise the thoughts need the body to clothe themselves and to draw material for their activity. Without feelings and thoughts the body is dead, without the body you cannot feel, and without feelings you cannot think, indeed without the body, thoughts and feelings are not present for us. But when these components have once found their accord and interaction, then the duration of the human is as certain as the primal powers of the universe.

But how do we arrive at this accord? How can the thoughts merge with the body? Does the body not preclude all power of thought? The answer to these questions occupies me incessantly. Light with all its colours is spread throughout the entire earth, and just so must thoughts also fill the body. What now are the colours or the elements of thinking? The answer: speech, numbers, and forms. Through your entire body you must learn to count, create forms, and speak; then world history and your own existence will become clear to you."

They made their way out of the shaft. When they stepped into daylight again, Mohrland said, "Am I right, that here in the warm sunlight it is more beautiful than below?" Silbert's thoughts were occupied with the beings of Greek mythology,

---

*   [Tr.: orcus is Latin for death.]

whereat he at once received the key. "There is light everywhere," he said spontaneously to Mohrland's question, "but we do not suspect it, seek it, or know it. You gave me below the earth much material for making light, and in thanks I will endeavour to ignite it."

The day passed quickly in the contemplation of the beauty of nature and amidst conversations about the nature and effects of it on all life circumstances.

On the third day, Mohrland gave his guests a small celebration in which, however, apart from them nobody took part. It was for Silbert a great pleasure to hear for the first time outpourings of the heart which sprung from the core of life, grasped our inner being, and as it were animated it anew. Mohrland abandoned himself entirely to his feelings and poured over things of great importance for the encouragement and strengthening of his new friend. At the conclusion, he grasped each of them, one with his right, the other with his left hand, and said, "We have found ourselves, we do not want to lose ourselves anymore. In eternity there is a point about which everything turns. Outside is the storm, at the point, at the axis there is calm. We stand in the centre, and even if the world may turn in fury, we will seek immortality, and in this feeling we remain happy and strong.

The following day, they parted from Mohrland with the promise of visiting him once more in a year's time. Fielding went back to his work and sought to catch up on what he had neglected. Silbert, however, returned full of great enthusiasm to his farmstead in order to think, to act, and to practise according to Mohrland's instructions.

The task hovered continuously in his head. "The entire body should learn to count, create forms, and speak. Until in the deepest part of the earth, the light of heaven penetrates, and creates colours and forms. Well! He set on her feet that girl tormented by spirits. The feet are a part of the body, are its pillars; with these I want to make a start."

He also continued his other exercises with great eagerness. He saw indeed almost that the new task made the previous one superfluous, because by nature everything was contained in the latter, but he did not have the courage to forgo it, and so he plied it amidst alternate visits to Fielding for five months. But now the moment seemed to have come when a new crisis arose and it had to be decided whether nature would unveil its secrets to him or not.

One day he went to his friend quite disturbed. "I cannot continue," he said, "my power abandons me. Monsters that are not found in visible creation are acting against me. I possess courage, but here I succumb when such forces conspire against me. Help me, for without your assistance I am lost!"

Fielding seized his hand and felt a fierce heat in his friend's veins. The eyes zipped back and forth as if he were frightened of letting them rest on a spot; the lips trembled and seemed to want to speak, but the words remained timidly in the mouth. "Get a hold of yourself," Fielding said, "everything will turn out alright. If the enemies do not show themselves, they cannot attack you. So courage!"

Silbert replied, "It is an eternity! I have seen your realm; whether I will arrive there, however, I doubt. My life has been split. On my skin there is a wild fire so that I often imagine I am wandering in a fever. In my innards it is billowing like a sea. My heart has left me, for in it alone I feel no life anymore, but it rages all the more violently in my brain. The roar of spirits, the bellowing of dogs, satanic debates where the most revealed truths are turned into lies, fire and night images reveal themselves to me and chase me when I just abandon myself to myself. Yes, while I am speaking with you, I am not free of such ghosts, and I feel that this state goes beyond my physical powers because I cannot sleep anymore and nothing refreshes me."

Fielding told him to stay and reside with him for as long as until the crisis was over. "I must observe your condition myself," he said, "so that I can specify the safe means against it."

Towards evening, they were both sitting alone in the garden. At once Silbert's voice obtained a strength as if he had to speak into the greatest distance. Fielding asked, "Why are you so vehement, my friend?"

Silbert: An inner violence is forcing me.

Fielding: Stay master of it.

Silbert: I am barely in control of it. It is urging me to call out into the world that all teaching is vain and possesses the blindness of the regiment.

Fielding: Who is saying that in you?

Silbert: Not me, it is another who is in me though and gives me the words which I must express almost against my will.

Fielding: The advocate does not want to lose his crown and is seeking to overwhelm you.

Silbert: A gentle thought is in the background, that I can well feel, but I cannot abide his words, for they penetrate all my nerves; yes, I believe they are touching the marrow of my bones. Then I see, but only for moments, a new heaven from which it flows like the breath of life.

Fielding: That heaven is your goal; to learn to gaze at it calmly, our striving is for that. What you see between you and that heaven are the obstacles which God and nature have placed in order to bar the entrance to the sinner, the weakling, the idler. The fire is the flaming sword which defends the entrance to paradise, the bellowing is of Cerberus who frightens away those approaching, all the worms and monsters you see are Furies and Eumenides who threaten to mistreat us and destroy us before we reach Elysium. You must go into battle against these apparitions, against this world of images, under whatever forms they approximate, and dispel them; then you will enter paradise where eternal heaven resides, where pure knowledge illuminates, where nothing more disturbs the peace, but instead truth in the purest gleam as the law of life fills, lights and guides us.

Silbert felt emboldened by this talk, and said, "Thank you and I give my word not to rest before I have obtained victory and scared off all my doubts, even if they are veiled in such terrible figures."

He kept his word. He only had to struggle for five full months before he obtained calm again. A few times the screaming monster overwhelmed his entire being so much that he was not master of his expressions anymore, and even emitted violent words towards his friend. On such occasions, Feilding remained completely calm and said at most, "More power to you! Always to you so that you will soon fly away with your words into the air! The demon is seeing his approaching downfall and raging in a last exertion of strength. Let him rage, and call on the eternal thoughts for help."

Silbert did so and saw that his vision cleared up and peace was established again in his inner being.

Once he said, when he was walking up and down with his friend in the garden, "It is getting lively in my heart. It prickles even when the proper spark of life penetrates, but I feel that there a main source of our powers is flowing and I am obtaining myself with its possession."

"So it is," Fielding answered. "There is the centre of the star which you often catch sight of, but which has not yet connected with you. It will move ever closer until it fills you, illuminates you, and shows you in all the radiance of its circle a life force which streams uninterruptedly into us and forms us thereby into a complete whole for which nature supplies the nourishment according to immutable laws, indeed, it must supply it!"

Silbert continued his activity, ever since he caught sight of such results, with doubled zeal, and paid little attention anymore to the phenomena which fluttered about him on all sides. But fierce struggle still awaited him. The tendency to doubt acted against him once more, and before his inner eye a new, glowing figure of deception formed. A master of desires awoke in him, which he previously barely knew by name. Fielding in this crisis called on Mohrland for help, and said to him when arrived, "Our friend stands before the door to life, give him the courage to enter."

They went to Silbert. When he caught sight of Mohrland, he seemed more frightened than joyed; but he pulled himself together and bade him welcome.

Mohrland saw the awkwardness of his behaviour and said, "Why so timid, my friend? I hoped to find you calm and happy, and now I see you agitated, in conflict with yourself."

Silbert wiped his forehead and looked at him disconcertingly, as if woken from a sleep. "You find me," he now said, "in a strange state. I have gained what I never dared hope, and yet I cannot renounce all doubt. Why do they let the heart go out in our youth so unguardedly into the world of hypotheses in whose snares the better feelings become entangled and finally lose all strength. Now I see and yet cannot yet believe because the doubt in me has grown up into vital powers whose weapons work more powerfully than my newly awakened attitudes."

Mohrland: I know your state. Your heart is not yet open. The thoughts of that new heaven are too distant from your usual intellectual powers for them to be able to consolidate themselves so quickly. But just be brave! The victory will not stay away much longer. With such fundamental doubters as you, knowledge and experience must go hand in hand so that the feelings can raise themselves to their peculiar power. Principles are not suited to your position, lively images or parables taken from life are alone capable of giving you the necessary firmness. Hence listen to a small story:

"Among the acquaintances of my youth was found one by the name of Lehwald, with an unusually sharp eye, both for close-up and at a distance. He could not comprehend how humans could be so foolish to make glasses, perspectives, and telescopes in order to see better. 'Every material,' he said, 'and even if it is the purest glass, condenses the air and interrupts the radiation of light, hence they cannot possibly show the object to the eye any clearer.' One indeed explained to him the refraction of beams of light, the properties of convex and concave glass, the narrowing of light in the lens and so on; but he stuck to it — he could not comprehend and did not believe either that behind that small lens the objects were enlarged.

Thus it is with you. You cannot imagine how it is possible to direct the senses to spiritual objects; but it is the same case as with the visible glasses. Our physical eye is too dull for divine visions, we must therefore accustom ourselves to directing them through our body, through our life parts, to make there a perspective, and to gaze through a lens behind which all supernatural objects are to be recognised in complete clarity like the earthly through a telescope. Indeed, even more; in the kingdom of life it is not only the eye that forms its lens, but rather all senses form their lens, and hearing, seeing, smelling, tasting, feeling, even speaking receive thereby thoughts of which the common human has no idea and hence declares them, like the acquaintance of my youth, to be nonsense. Make this allegory clear to yourself, then you will find that it gives you a strength against the doubt and those wild phenomena which arise in the consciousness, and delivers to you every day new weapons for defence, then finally for attack, and in the end for victory."

Silbert had listened to this allegory with great interest. "I want to seek the lens," he said, "and if the images of doubt appear, to see them at once in their true form; then I will perhaps gain the advantage over them and be able to banish them from my circle."

With fresh vigour, he went again to his researches. He obtained the skillfulness in all parts of his body, from the toes to the top of his head, of forming a lens and gazing at everything he wanted to in its true form. Seventeen weeks passed in this exercise, then he said to Fielding, "I do not need any supervision anymore, and if it continues thus, I hope in a short time to force through every obstacle, and to enter into the long yearned for new heaven."

He went again to the farmstead, and unhitched himself for one more year from all public business in order to obtain by uninterrupted practice more and more firmness. It was turning out wonderfully in him, he gazed into the future and into the distance. The keys to all knowledge became his by and by, and after the elapse of a year he felt strong enough to step again into bourgeois life. He revealed to his two friends this decision. Fielding was doubtful, but Mohrland said, "It may occur, but the interrupted area of activity must be begun only slowly, otherwise you run the danger of coming to a stop halfway and thereby doing yourself harm instead of good." Silbert promised extreme caution and vowed to obey in his future life course the laws of the spirit, and to give every year an account over his activity.

Mohrland's mood reached a high degree of solemnity when Silbert offered him his hand with intimate thanks and took his leave. "You have found," he said, "what so few are granted. Eternity has unlocked itself for you, and immortality is no puzzle for you anymore. Yet more is to be achieved if you remain steadfast, for a new world has been unlocked for you in which you can now gather experience. The world of illusions lies in part already behind you, now you are entering into a new realm where no figures appear to you, where everything stands in semi-darkness before you; there it must become day, there new images must come to light which no longer deceive, but instead, being formed from the purest light, indicate and speak only truth. Thus if new doubts approach you in the future, then turn yourself to there; there in that unalterable light the spirits of those who have gone before will reveal themselves to you and give you full explanations. Farewell, in a year we will see each other again!"

After the passage of the stated time, they arrived together again, and Silbert took up the conversation, "The legal work did not want to get going, hence I have kept myself up to now away from all business." His friends approved this approach and rejoiced at his progress in the art of inspecting eternity.

***

The New Heaven

Four times he arrived in this way, as it were as a student. The last time, however, he gave such information that Mohrland solemnly exclaimed, "He is complete! Now he may do what his heart desires, it will never lead him astray."

Silbert, when he gave news of himself, told of amongst other things, "The spiritual world has been unlocked for me; everything which I desired to know from earlier times, I learn through those who took part in them. Even my late father comes as often as I wish, guides and teaches me over the most difficult affairs. I have obtained what you laid down for me when you said, 'If you do not believe the living, then you may ask the dead.' The dead live, they reveal themselves to me, they give me answers, and with this the path to immortality is transformed."

"He is transformed," Mohrland said; "we are united and already live on the other side in the here and now. You are ours, you are one with us, and with this the circle is closed. We are of one heart and of one mind; we will never lose each other, even if the visible sun vanishes and a new creation ousts the current one. Brother Fielding, let us live the joy! Treat us today as guests of a better land in which holiness is paired with the purest cheerfulness."

It was a great celebration for all three. Silbert felt so exalted that he burst out in delight, "Now I recognise what it means to reside in heaven! Such feelings as I feel today can only come from the other side because only there is calm possible with the full activity of life. I feel as if I were dissolved in love and bliss, whilst a power prevails in me which I never felt before, which my ego vouches for and secures from all dissolution. Eternity reigns in me, the brilliance of the creator which stands above all that is transitory radiates again in my heart; I think the entire creation mirrors itself in my inner being and exults with me in an eternal hallelujah to the throne of the almighty."

Amidst such outpourings and emotions, the day drew to an end. The next morning they parted with the joyful consciousness of living as one in the other's spirit, wherever external circumstances should lead them. Mohrland went to his shaft, Fielding to his calculations, and Silbert only now undertook again all the business which offered itself to him in his profession, and achieved through the unveiling of the most confused affairs such a reputation that people came from distant lands and asked him for advice.

***

Comparisons with the Bible

Just as truth is eternal, so is the human who has recognised the truth in his inner being.

Only a few seek in themselves, and hence they remain distant from the conviction of an eternal duration. They presume to claim or to contradict with mere words, but do not acquire the living feeling, and hence they cannot raise themselves to belief.

Anyone who cannot believe in immortality must make detours to come to certainty, and hence it does not annoy any true believer that in the present treatise vaguer means have also been used to guide those seeking towards the goal.

"Strive for the conception of the spirit, for the rebirth in the spirit," is the doctrine of all wisdom, all religions, and especially our sublime Christian religion whose founder himself said:

> Mark 3
> 28: Verily I say unto you, All sins shall be forgiven unto the sons of men, and blasphemies wherewith soever they shall blaspheme:
> 29: But he that shall blaspheme against the Holy Ghost hath never forgiveness, but is in danger of eternal damnation.

This idea lies at the base of the above treatise. To seek the traces of the spirit, to awaken it, to draw it forth under the veils of the flesh and the vanities of the world, Mohrland uses any means because he knows that you investigate everything and can obtain everything through the spirit, but without it the life of the human is a dead grain which will never germinate, much less bear the fruits of eternity.

Fielding, Mohrland's student, to begin with attempted everything to bring the one thirsting for truth to the goal through the doctrine of faith, but it bounced off the bark of wordly wisdom and scepticism, and so he had to have his apprentice wander through all the threads of life; he had to first ignite the immortal flame in him and stoke it up, before that one could arrive at a conviction of faith.

Faith is certainly a foundation pillar of Christianity, but it must lead to the recognition of the spirit, to the rebirth, otherwise it is an evil, a false seed from which evil, superstition, and confusion arise. Humans can accustom themselves to believe foolish, even absurd things; the faith of Christianity on the other hand demands awakening of the spirit which unveils the truth to us.

There are people who believe the fables of Indian folk tales, but they impersonate the spirit and would like to use it for worldly adventures; as a result they achieve nothing and head towards the visible death. Faith in an eternity, in an eternal providence, in a salvation in the flesh, is the indispensable condition if we want to arrive at the place where Christ directed the faithful.

Christ gives us in addition to faith two other life powers for winning immortality, or, as he calls it, the kingdom of heaven, hope and love.

Anyone who yearns for immortality, loves it, and will in the end find its spirit in themselves.

Anyone who loves immortality desires; whoever desires for something for a long time, in the end hopes for it. Love and hope produce the inner human which finally comes to life in us in the complete power of faith.

The Christian religion leads us at first by glorious principles, through teaching the love of eternity, that is, and completes its work through the powers of faith.

Faith is the infallible seed from which the fullness of all life, of all happiness and immortality emerges.

The propositions themselves which Christ expressed about this life power are so heart-lifting, so practical and clear that you often must wonder why you so rarely see their use, and why Christianity languishes in constant ignorance, in fear and doubt, in sorrow and misery, in struggle and argument, in poverty and sickness, since help against all evil is contained in the strength of faith.

Through what reader does sacred delight not glow when they read such verses which give them complete security against all trouble through faith.

Matthew 8

5: And when Jesus was entered into Capernaum, there came unto him a centurion, beseeching him,

6: And saying, Lord, my servant lieth at home sick of the palsy, grievously tormented.

7: And Jesus saith unto him, I will come and heal him.

8: The centurion answered and said, Lord, I am not worthy that thou shouldest come under my roof: but speak the word only, and my servant shall be healed.

10: When Jesus heard it, he marvelled, and said to them that followed, Verily I say unto you, I have not found so great faith, no, not in Israel.

13: And Jesus said unto the centurion, Go thy way; and as thou hast believed, so be it done unto thee. And his servant was healed in the selfsame hour.

24: And, behold, there arose a great tempest in the sea, insomuch that the ship was covered with the waves: but he was asleep.

25: And his disciples came to him, and awoke him, saying, Lord, save us: we perish.

26: And he saith unto them, Why are ye fearful, O ye of little faith? Then he arose, and rebuked the winds and the sea; and there was a great calm.

Matthew 9

2: And, behold, they brought to him a man sick of the palsy, lying on a bed: and Jesus seeing their faith said unto the sick of the palsy; Son, be of good cheer; thy sins be forgiven thee.

27: And when Jesus departed thence, two blind men followed him, crying, and saying, Thou son of David, have mercy on us.

28: And when he was come into the house, the blind men came to him: and Jesus saith unto them, Believe ye that I am able to do this? They said unto him, Yea, Lord.

29: Then touched he their eyes, saying, According to your faith be it unto you.

30: And their eyes were opened; and Jesus straitly charged them, saying, See that no man know it.

Matthew 21

20: And when the disciples saw it, they marvelled, saying, How soon is the fig tree withered away!

21: Jesus answered and said unto them, Verily I say unto you, If ye have faith, and doubt not, ye shall not only do this which is done to the fig tree, but also if ye shall say unto this mountain, Be thou removed, and be thou cast into the sea; it shall be done.

22: And all things, whatsoever ye shall ask in prayer, believing, ye shall receive.

Mark 5

25: And a certain woman, which had an issue of blood twelve years,

26: And had suffered many things of many physicians, and had spent all that she had, and was nothing bettered, but rather grew worse,

27: When she had heard of Jesus, came in the press behind, and touched his garment.

28: For she said, If I may touch but his clothes, I shall be whole.

29: And straightway the fountain of her blood was dried up; and she felt in her body that she was healed of that plague.

34: And he said unto her, Daughter, thy faith hath made thee whole; go in peace, and be whole of thy plague.

Mark 6

5: And he could there do no mighty work, save that he laid his hands upon a few sick folk, and healed them.

6: And he marvelled because of their unbelief.

It is easy to see that here it is referring to a different sort of belief than we see in common life, and of which the scholars only seek the literal meaning. Faith here is a power which raises itself to the awareness of life and fills us with a divine light.

When humans believe truly, they are conscious of this activity just like they are of the efficacy of other life urges, and seek contentment in exchange.

It is not blind faith that is meant here, but rather that conviction which we feel and has become alive in us.

Every activity has its goal in which the test of it is contained. When the goal is reached, the activity was good, when it is not reached, then we are in error.

The goal of faith is production of an eternal life in us which renews the human and calls him in the rebirth to the proper existence.

Anyone who does not distinctly recognise and sense the reborn within themselves does not have it, as much as they might also read, write, and speak about it.

The reading of the Bible is not the task, but rather that we arrive at its meaning, place this meaning within ourselves as a seed, and plant ourselves for the word of God and for eternity.

The Bible is a work of the holy spirit, but it is not the spirit itself. They are thus very much in error when the Bible is everything to them; it must merely guide us and we must find the teachings from it confirmed in us practically.

Anyone who then believes the word of God is in the Bible believes correctly; but anyone who thinks this belief is sufficient deceives themselves and perishes because they are not seeking the living spirit within themselves.

The Bible shows us the way; Christ is our model. To that we shall strive to change and to imitate him in all associations of our lives and in all circumstances.

To fulfil the commands of Christ is good; but all his teachings for our conduct are only the preparations for the higher goal, for the conception of the spirit and for the rebirth.

Anyone who wants to rightly bear the name of Christian must arrive in the spirit; anyone who shimmers in the outer knowledge, who proves the propositions of holy scripture only through other texts in it, they turn around in a circle whose centre they never find.

Christ speaks openly about the necessity of the rebirth.

John 3

1: There was a man of the Pharisees, named Nicodemus, a ruler of the Jews:

2: The same came to Jesus by night, and said unto him, Rabbi, we know that thou art a teacher come from God: for no man can do these miracles that thou doest, except God be with him.

3: Jesus answered and said unto him, Verily, verily, I say unto thee, Except a man be born again, he cannot see the kingdom of God.

4: Nicodemus saith unto him, How can a man be born when he is old? can he enter the second time into his mother's womb, and be born?

5: Jesus answered, Verily, verily, I say unto thee, Except a man be born of water and of the Spirit, he cannot enter into the kingdom of God.

To be reproduced by the spirit and reborn in it remains the unalterable instruction of our sublime religion, and it is only to be regretted that this basic truth is so frequently overlooked, and instead of reinforcing it practically, is practised with quotations and argumentation.

By what does the human recognise the rebirth? Answer: By his way of life, when it changes and passes from the transient to the eternal.

From the change in his attitude, if he only has desire for the eternal and unchangeable, and considers everything transient to be a stage in which he can test, gather, and reform himself.

By the new senses which are revealed in him, by which he also perceives things which are invisible, hears sounds, notes, and words which do not come from any human mouth, indeed, finds renewed all the organs in his inner being, by which he gazes into eternity, and there draws experiences and knowledge.

I know that here there are some who do not believe, but that does not alter the matter one iota; an eternal life is yet present, is in us, and reveals itself when we earnestly seek.

Matthew 7
7: Ask, and it shall be given you; seek, and ye shall find; knock, and it shall be opened unto you:
8: For every one that asketh receiveth; and he that seeketh findeth; and to him that knocketh it shall be opened.

In these three commands lies the freedom and power to obtain everything. Anyone who seeks incessantly, prays uninterruptedly, and knocks daily, indeed often hourly at the gates of eternity, finds and obtains what they pray for, and wins entry to eternity in their visible body.

Christ calls us to the kingdom of God, to the kingdom of heaven; the entry to the spirit, to the new life, is also the entry to the kingdom of heaven.

Luke 17
20: And when he was demanded of the Pharisees, when the kingdom of God should come, he answered them and said, The kingdom of God cometh not with observation:
21: Neither shall they say, Lo here! or, lo there! for, behold, the kingdom of God is within you.

We must win the kingdom of heaven in the here and now, after death we lack the means for it. We must draw from the flesh the spirit which comes from God, we can never obtain it elsewhere. Or do you believe it comes unbidden, it announces itself without effort and sacrifice? That is unthinkable, for even the evil spirits do not arrive in us when we do not call them, do not open to them.

Humans certainly have many talents for sin, but they would never have grown so terrible if we did not nurse them, through guile and leisure, through immorality and haughtiness, through ambition and arrogance, through obloquy and embezzlement, etc. But when we devote ourselves to just one of these satellites of hell, it opens the doors and gates to the others.

But fortunately it is also so with the human virtues — anyone who makes a great effort to cultivate only one of them, love, loyalty, fear of God, humility, moderation, morality, truth, etc., into them by and by all the virtues come, and then the gates to eternal wisdom open so that it illuminates us already in the here and now and strengthens us with invincible powers.

We are getting closer to the matter which we wanted to explain, and find that you cannot arrive so easily at true faith as many suspect. The prescribed ceremonies are not truths of faith, they are only means to obtain it. These ceremonies may also deviate from one another, and if we do not forget the goal of arriving in the spirit, then we are nevertheless safe.

In our example cited above, the teacher could not even use the Christian principles because his student had no sense for them anymore, and he was therefore required to penetrate into his inner being and awaken the spirit on different, partly Greek mythological paths. Now I ask, did he do evil by that?

Answer: No, he could not do anything else.

Question: But will it not irritate Christians?

Answer: If they are rational — no.

Question: How must there mind be then?

Answer: They must think that God is present in all beings. To acknowledge him, to awaken his spirit in us, is the task; if this is done, then the first duty of the Christian is fulfilled.

Question: But if you are suggesting this could only happen in a Christian way?

Answer: It is also thus proper if we first give those who are seeking the ability to seek such paths; but if they do not have this, then it must be awoken and brought forth. The unbeliever is a child whom you must educate before you can utilise it for a business, be it even so small. You must, however, treat any child according to its abilities, then it learns and is to be educated; if you proceed differently, then it becomes obdurate and often remains spoilt for their entire life. Are we permitted to reproach Fielding for proceeding with Silbert in the same way? —

***

Christ is the son of God. But he did not want to come to humanity as such, but in order to give them a model of how high they stand before God in the hierarchy of creation. Christ acted not as the son of God, but as a human in order to teach us to obtain the kingdom of heaven, to ennoble us for a better life, and to free us from all the tribulations of the short earthly existence.

Above we have shown the powers of faith. Now we enter the circle of eternity where the spirit works with spirits, and affects them or is affected by them as the circumstances demand.

Christ conquered everything by faith and taught humanity how this power works. But he stood higher yet through his direct contact with the eternal powers of nature, with angels and spirits, and became for us thereby the undeniable model of immortality in that he obtained instruction from them and also from those long dead.

We see also in his story, as in the above, a key difference of the spirit phenomena in that the one only affects subordinately, but others prove to be from the kingdom of heaven, in complete purity.

The hellish or evil spirits are products of our perverse life's desires, and prepare in us also a rebirth which, however, arises from evil seeds.

All that humans pursue and do with zeal comes to live in them and assumes dominance in them. Language, form, movement, and everything becomes subordinate to this force so that it finally possesses us entirely and thinks and acts in our ego.

Anyone who lets this new evil ego calmly prevail is led by it with cleverness and acumen through life, and they are finally accustomed to trust only earthly powers, and by contrast consider eternal properties and influences to be folk tales.

Such humans can only rise with effort to a sham faith, the power of which, however, is constantly closed to them. Contact with spirits is to them preposterous, an impossibility, and for any allusion to it they have an objection which is given to them without their knowing by the evil spirit produced in them. The quick gift of contradicting increases their obduracy in that they delight in the shimmer of their contradictions and consider it to be a result of extreme rationality.

In our days it has come so far that faithless and rational are one and the same thing. But then as a result even doctors and philosophers no longer know how to help with the slightest spiritual phenomenon.

Silbert made the conviction of the immortality of humanity his task. He could not obtain this with his emotional state and with the constant urge to doubt in any other way than by putting himself in contact with immortal spirits. His teacher saw this and followed their plan accordingly. Only after they dislodged all that was extraneous from him, or to speak as per the Bible, drove out all the evil spirits from him, and had reproduced in him the original human nature, could they succeed in leading him to the new heaven or to the kingdom of heaven where he caught sight of new forms and among these the spirit of his father.

To begin with he saw larvae and ghosts who tormented and obstructed him; only with effort and endeavour did he succeed in disposing of this evil company. We catch sight of the same phenomena with Caroline Ruppert who without help would have succumbed to her evil influences.

Even Christ called these powers spirits and devils, as if they were something outside of us, something separate. This must not lead us astray, however, for according to their effect they are something outside of us in that they, particularly when they must leave us, part from us as bodily beings and only forcibly; according to the nature of the matter, however, they were one with us, were spiritual outgrowths which must be detached from us in order to bring us again into complete unity with ourselves.

The purified human stands there as a complete unity and nothing can tarnish his inner being anymore. The obdurate human is also a complete unity and bristles against the dissolution which sooner or later must take place in his inner being. This dissolution expresses itself visibly through dream images, through a sort of madness, or through spirit phenomena. The first type is unanswerable because all humans experience them. The second is placed under the class of physical illnesses, and one also seeks to heal it with physical means. The third belongs amongst the disreputable things which are reproached with the clearest features as swindles or self-deception.

Unusual fates, misfortune, remorse, even fear of death sometimes shake the obduracy of humans and awaken powers in them which are contrary to their usual state; a struggle follows, the former passions and desires rise into images and contend for possession of their master, and thus it can occur that the number of such phenomena becomes legion. If you feel in such a position a capability in yourself to reinforce the better, pure nature and to raise it to its office, then by and by those images will flee, and the previously plagued human will emerge from this struggle as someone reborn to whom heaven is revealed and angels themselves sing songs of praise.

The stories cited above take this course, and Christ treated the possessed and those tormented by evil spirits just the same.

In order to reinforce this, I want to look at some of his works in this relation and at the same time hear his words over them.

Matthew 8

> 16: When the even was come, they brought unto him many that were possessed with devils: and he cast out the spirits with his word, and healed all that were sick:

> 28: And when he was come to the other side into the country of the Gergesenes, there met him two possessed with devils, coming out of the tombs, exceeding fierce, so that no man might pass by that way.
> 29: And, behold, they cried out, saying, What have we to do with thee, Jesus, thou Son of God? art thou come hither to torment us before the time?
> 30: And there was a good way off from them an herd of many swine feeding.
> 31: So the devils besought him, saying, If thou cast us out, suffer us to go away into the herd of swine.
> 32: And he said unto them, Go. And when they were come out, they went into the herd of swine: and, be-

hold, the whole herd of swine ran violently down a steep place into the sea, and perished in the waters.

Matthew 10

7: And as ye go, preach, saying, The kingdom of heaven is at hand.

8: Heal the sick, cleanse the lepers, raise the dead, cast out devils: freely ye have received, freely give.

Matthew 15

22: And, behold, a woman of Canaan came out of the same coasts, and cried unto him, saying, Have mercy on me, O Lord, thou son of David; my daughter is grievously vexed with a devil.

28: Then Jesus answered and said unto her, O woman, great is thy faith: be it unto thee even as thou wilt. And her daughter was made whole from that very hour.

Matthew 17

14: And when they were come to the multitude, there came to him a certain man, kneeling down to him, and saying,

15: Lord, have mercy on my son: for he is lunatick, and sore vexed: for ofttimes he falleth into the fire, and oft into the water.

16: And I brought him to thy disciples, and they could not cure him.

17: Then Jesus answered and said, O faithless and perverse generation, how long shall I be with you? how long shall I suffer you? bring him hither to me.

18: And Jesus rebuked the devil; and he departed out of him: and the child was cured from that very hour.

19: Then came the disciples to Jesus apart, and said, Why could not we cast him out?

20: And Jesus said unto them, Because of your unbelief: for verily I say unto you, If ye have faith as a grain of mustard seed, ye shall say unto this mountain, Remove hence to yonder place; and it shall remove; and nothing shall be impossible unto you.

Mark 1

23: And there was in their synagogue a man with an unclean spirit; and he cried out,

24: Saying, Let us alone; what have we to do with thee, thou Jesus of Nazareth? art thou come to destroy us? I know thee who thou art, the Holy One of God.

25: And Jesus rebuked him, saying, Hold thy peace, and come out of him.

26: And when the unclean spirit had torn him, and cried with a loud voice, he came out of him.

32: And at even, when the sun did set, they brought unto him all that were diseased, and them that were possessed with devils.

33: And all the city was gathered together at the door.

34: And he healed many that were sick of divers diseases, and cast out many devils; and suffered not the devils to speak, because they knew him.

We see from the texts cited how precisely the spirits of the holy scripture conform with Mohrland's manner of treatment because we encounter them connected everywhere with the characteristics of the person to the smallest detail, and they must as it were be considered to be spiritual outgrowths which have become powerful through their extent. They have inner knowledge and know exactly that Christ has power over them and who he is.

But with all these powers, with all these phenomena, immortality was not yet clearly proven, and hence Mohrland guided his student through the entire host of phenomena in order to finally make him capable of seeing the new heaven and gathering knowledge there.

In the Bible, especially in the Old Testament, there are a number of examples of those who have achieved such directness with the eternal; but we will content ourselves with selecting a few from the New Testament here in order to give the reader the ready means to enquire further.

Matthew 17

1: And after six days Jesus taketh Peter, James, and John his brother, and bringeth them up into an high mountain apart,

2: And was transfigured before them: and his face did shine as the sun, and his raiment was white as the light.

3: And, behold, there appeared unto them Moses and Elias talking with him.

4: Then answered Peter, and said unto Jesus, Lord, it is good for us to be here: if thou wilt, let us make here three tabernacles; one for thee, and one for Moses, and one for Elias.

5: While he yet spake, behold, a bright cloud overshadowed them: and behold a voice out of the cloud, which said, This is my beloved Son, in whom I am well pleased; hear ye him.

Luke 1

11: And there appeared unto him an angel of the Lord standing on the right side of the altar of incense.

12: And when Zacharias saw him, he was troubled, and fear fell upon him.

13: But the angel said unto him, Fear not, Zacharias: for thy prayer is heard; and thy wife Elisabeth shall bear thee a son, and thou shalt call his name John.

18: And Zacharias said unto the angel, Whereby shall I know this? for I am an old man, and my wife well stricken in years.

19: And the angel answering said unto him, I am Gabriel, that stand in the presence of God; and am sent to speak unto thee, and to shew thee these glad tidings.

20: And, behold, thou shalt be dumb, and not able to speak, until the day that these things shall be performed, because thou believest not my words, which shall be fulfilled in their season.

Comparisons with the Bible

These few may be enough here. Anyone who wants to read more, look in the Pentateuch of the Old Testament, in the prophets, and in the later history of Israel and you will bump into examples of this class everywhere.

To vanquish death is the highest task which Christ gave the human race. But here many come into doubt and suggest such a thing is possible for the son of God, but that the natural human must not think of such perfection.

I repeat once more: Christ is given to humanity as the model; what he did, humans shall also do; what he accomplished, humans can also accomplish.

Here you are astounded, and many will accuse me of exaggeration, probably even of blasphemy. But I am building on the text that all will be forgiven, only the sins against the spirit will not, and seek this and speak to it the truths which are infallible because they come from it.*

Christ is our model. To imitate him is our duty. Now I ask: in which way do you imitate him?

You do as he did.

Question: That is succinctly put, but how is it possible?

Answer: The spirit helps. Anyone who does not have it is a lost member and cannot comprehend the work at all, much less do it.

Question: What did Christ do?

Answer: He helped, where it was needed, through the power of the spirit; taught in the schools, healed the sick, awoke the dead, drove out devils, and finally robbed death of its sting.

Question: But if everyone wanted to do all that, then always one would have to oust another, otherwise he would

---

*   [Tr.: cf. Matthew 12:31–32: Wherefore I say unto you, All manner of sin and blasphemy shall be forgiven unto men: but the blasphemy against the Holy Ghost shall not be forgiven unto men. / And whosoever speaketh a word against the Son of man, it shall be forgiven him: but whosoever speaketh against the Holy Ghost, it shall not be forgiven him, neither in this world, neither in the world to come.
Mark 3:28–29: Verily I say unto you, All sins shall be forgiven unto the sons of men, and blasphemies wherewith soever they shall blaspheme: / But he that shall blaspheme against the Holy Ghost hath never forgiveness, but is in danger of eternal damnation.]

have nobody to teach, to heal, to awaken, in short, social life would have to be formed entirely differently?

Answer: It is true everybody would be taught by the spirit, illnesses would disappear, and death would be banished from earth. Would that be so bad then?!

∗∗∗

Overview

The paths to immortality are specified by certain phenomena of nature; whether they will suffice, the result will show. — We have looked at the matter, even if not exhaustively, from such undeniable effects though that anyone for whom it is do with conviction can make their own observations and inquire in themselves.

The methods which are given in the letters were regarded by the most ancient nations as signposts, and were sufficient for them because they still kept the feeling of immortality alive in themselves. In our times, when wordy erudition has supplanted almost all inner feeling, they no longer suffice, and we encounter in every society those such as Silbert who would like to know the matter instead of believing it. We thus want in this respect to survey the principles of the given examples and teaching once more, and to elucidate the consequences of it in the most concise manner possible.

Silbert cannot believe; the feeling of religiosity has died in him, even the love for life has subsided in its effects so that he no longer acknowledges and feels the root and the aim of it; in this state he enters the school of his friend who undertakes to awaken his spiritual life and to obtain for it the mastery over the outer life.

The first spiritual perceptions to which he is directed are the images of dream. Here you marvel with him and cannot comprehend how such everyday phenomena can serve as foundation pillars for the most important teaching, the teaching of immortality. But we must admire precisely therein the love of the creative primal force, that it places the first proof so close to us and continuously invites us thereby to enter its school.

Dreams, you say, are illusions, and hence no proof for the truth of a doctrine; dreams are illusions, this cannot be contradicted, but they are at the same time images whose existence too nobody can deny. Hence it is safer to build on them than on the usual conclusions which which you compose as per the school, filling the head with them, but leaving our feelings cold.

Dreams have among the usual researchers therefore no value because no objectivity is contained in them, or according to the common idiom, because the object of which you dream is not touched. E.g., if a person appears to us in dream, then they know nothing of it, and from that you infer the inapplicability of reasoning by such phenomena. But, since the spirit sees everything in its own light, in images which it creates itself, this reproach loses all content because precisely thereby the independence of the spiritual activity is preserved in that it is capable of drawing everything from itself.

I do not know whether I am speaking clearly enough here, or whether you can yet make shady moves in order to attack the first degree of knowledge of a spiritual life; I mean, the matter is as clear as the sun, and hence we want to have everyone think for themselves about what they consider most expedient, and content ourselves with inviting those who declare the creations of dreams to be nothing to name for us a similar power which acts and creates with just such ease and animation, indeed, which contains everything within itself which belongs to life, as is the case with dreams.

The phenomena of dreams do not indeed give us any positive teaching for the common use of life, because they are still not outflows from our free will; they come and go without our doing, and nobody can say, today I want to dream this or that; we are bound in this respect, and must manage as it pleases the powers set in motion. But this does not take away from the capability any of its peculiar value; to the contrary, it reveals to us rather that it stands above us and does not care about our apparent will.

The powers of the inner life are constantly active, they need no rest, no recovery, and when humans align themselves with them at will, and are capable of seeing, hearing, and feeling their images, then they become our property, give us what we desire, and only then obtain truth and significance.

Dreams and free clairvoyance are the two endpoints of spiritual activity, and the doctrine of immortality of all the religions is based on this. The author started from this point of view with the above treatise, and has in all his examples given hints to recognise oneself in order to reach the desired goal.

Silbert, a stubborn sceptic, can not be led by any feeling, he wants to know and not to blindly believe, hence with him methods must be used which touch his outer organism from the inside out and place him in this way at a standpoint where he is led by experiences to knowledge, and by this first to faith.

It certainly seems to be a contradiction when you say experience leads to faith! But when we consider Silbert's story, we see that he was with complete conviction still compelled to faith because he could not bring the phenomena which were revealed to him into any other class of knowledge with all clarity, and had to suffice with the poverty of language in saying: "the powers which I recognise in me are of a spiritual nature and of the sort that I cannot doubt anymore their most intimate union with me and their eternal duration, but must believe them unconditionally."

The methods which were given for the achievement of his goal are so simple that nobody who does not make the attempt can believe in them, but anyone who does not shy from the effort and possesses the persistence will learn to see how far humans are from their spiritual ego, and what they obtain when they finally learn to call themselves into the innermost being of their heart.

The greatest part of the instruction revolves about this inner calling. It is indeed, after the bark has been broken through, divided into several grades, because humans also possess many powers, but they give this ego every time a different name in order to raise it to its highest dignity. We see the same procedure as well with Caroline Ruppert, only not to such an extended degree, because she, when Mohrland came to her, had already had many experiences in her inner being which were later of substantial use.

But I hear in spirit some reproaches here which you will make of this way of teaching. You will say, being foolish is not striding forwards on the path to life. If that were so, then you would have to wish to be born stupid in order to arrive at the goal sooner.

This reproach does not seem without basis; but yet it is only apparent. Humanity has two poles which stand opposite one another. Humans can live in the most perfect light entirely according to the laws of the spirit, in complete knowledge; but it is also possible that they consider darkness to be their element, and wander through their earthly existence in complete obduracy. At both of these poles, they are to a certain extent perfect, and form a complete unity in themselves. If now the one, be it from their own impulse, or compelled by unusual fate, is torn violently from their obduracy and comes through into the light, then it cannot occur any other way than that his entire nature is as it were thrown out of joint, and both spiritual and physical conditions occur which the usual psychologist cannot explain anymore, and they are placed under the class of some illness. If we could accompany the doctors in their rooms, then phenomena would be revealed to us which have their origin entirely in such a transition from obduracy to faith in a higher power and which are also not to be healed any differently than when you bring the capabilities of the soul into equilibrium with the body.

Everything forceful produces a hefty shock, so too the violent transition from night to truth. How gently by contrast was the inner life of the sailor and the captain awoken. How many childlike and pious souls do we get to know in everyday life who possess nothing but a calm faith, and when you test them exactly, their better life feels and perceives to the full extent. Everything in nature has its concordance and hence we must not be shocked if unusual phenomena meet us.

Humans have departed from the path and must turn around again in order to walk the right path. What they gathered from the wrong path has connected with their life and is not so easy to drive away or make inactive. Spiritual powers are in effect continuously, they create and shape words, thoughts, forms, and figures which, as we see in dreams, tease, love, and haunt us against our will. If we withdraw from the outer life a part of its influence, then it can easily happen that the put-aside powers portray images to us and make us hear words which lead us astray and cause us to fall out with ourselves for some time. Anyone who does not lose heart on such occasions and steadfastly follows their better goal vanquishes those hostile powers and hears finally words of life just as they see images of heaven.

The path to life goes through labyrinths. Happy those who find a thread which a loving hand placed in order to lead them more securely to the exit; they stroll with easy strides and have thereby already vanquished all monsters because they trusted the placed thread lovingly.

A star of heaven leads us from the darkness when our inner eye is awoken to life. Anyone who sees this star follows it confidently and is not to be tempted by the teaching of the day which ascribes such phenomena only to the blood, even often to the weather. Humans have a more certain guide in themselves who leads them through every mist and can only be dislodged by ourselves.

The allusion to Greek mythology gives us a clear view of how all the powers of nature penetrate themselves and affect each other. We see as it were with eyes how God excludes no creature from his heaven if it just to some extent makes an effort to seek and to recognise him. The three primal powers of the universe are called attention to here, of which each exists only for itself in the idea of the researcher, but in nature are never entirely separate. The earth is primal power and eternal, life likewise, so too God, who stands creatively over all, holds and rules it. Now our body may also perish, but the divine, which never parts, neither from the life nor from the body, is bound again with other matter in order to lead us to eternal life.

Body, life, and the divine, or according to our concepts the power of thought, is necessary for perfect life. We see from Mohrland's explanation how natural this union is, and have therefore nothing to do but to live the highest laws and to subordinate body and soul (life) to it in the most perfect concordance; then we are in heaven, and draw from the other two primal powers ever new nourishment for the eternal continuation.

Humans must possess themselves entirely, this is the goal of all doctrine, and Mohrland also seeks to lead his student there. Not only in heart or in head, no, humans must learn to feel and recognise themselves throughout their entire body, otherwise they mangle themselves and are not suitable for the perfect life.

Herein lies the awkwardness of humanity, which dedicates to a part of the body more holiness than the others, whereas they daily experience that no limb is useless and each must necessarily be present in order to fulfil the intentions of the creator.

Seek to preserve what you have and think, where life shows itself most clearly, there you are closest to God; but do not be partisan with your powers, and seize the conviction that the perfection must possess all powers.

In the deepest notes of music the higher notes are contained, hence climb down into the lowest chambers of your body and remember that Christ also descended into hell in order to call all souls and powers to life.

Do not rest until you have formed everywhere in yourself a lens through which you can view eternity, and do not be led astray if the world only makes demands on your head, and strives to fill it with every possible bit of knowledge for so long as until it threatens to separate from you and free itself from your feelings. Remain steadfast and keep yourself whole, otherwise you will be someone crucified, whose bones were broken on the cross, and hence may not be taken down anymore.

Trust the time and control the moment! This teaching is expressed in the above examples clearly; for years are required until humans reach the maturity where they discover the core of their life and can use it as guide.

Many will say the teachings are not usable because they require distancing from the world, even from their professional business. Anyone who can obtain their inner life in the world and alongside their professional business has no need to distance themselves from it; but anyone who despite their wishes and striving remains in the darkness, they must distance themselves from the obstacles which stand in their way if they do not want to renounce the future and themselves.

Yet happily for us, only a few earthly circumstances have a disturbing effect on the development of our new life, and therefore we want to be in charge of our profession with punctuality, give humanity an example of piety and love, and regard everything we do as done in God.

The life circumstances where our ambition, our acumen, or better shrewdness are demanded are those which are hardest to unite with the striving for spiritual truth, because they usually fill humans entirely and raise their characteristics to idols before which they stand blinded and honour them alone.

Business which can be performed with earnest diligence, with thoughtfulness, with calm consideration and thought power is not only not a hindrance, but often beneficial because it strives against a violent overthrowing of our nature, and draws everything onto the quiet track of our patience.

Hence nobody should be shocked before any one example, but should seek on their path the good which these teachings offer them. The inner and outer lives are always in the most exact agreement with each other. A delicate body will never yearn for the club of Hercules, a giant though will never play with violets, instead with tree trunks and cliffs. Thus in the realm of thoughts — ideas depend only on the possessor of them and alter their depiction as you transfer them into a different individual.

The aim of all life: seek the spirit in yourself, then you are safe. But seek your spirit, not another's. Herein lies a key problem with humanity, that they always depend on others and never give themselves a proper look. The spirit of another never becomes mine, it can merely illuminate me, even coming into my temple, but as little as I can implant and use the arm of another as my own, just as little do I allow the powers of the spirit to be enclosed in other forms. With water you can tune glasses to produce a chord; take the water out, pour it in other glasses, then you have no chord, and also none of the previous notes anymore. Everything you wish and desire must come from yourself; if you know this, learn it; rid yourself of all that is foreign, seek your ego, never the ego of another, only then is it possible to obtain the infallibility of life.

Harmony of the tones and mathematical forms are based on infallible principles and therefore cannot deceive; the harmony of your life must become as clear, being like the former based on unalterable laws and bearing its infallibility within itself.

Infallibility is our goal; everyone strives for infallibility, from the farmer to the highest scholar; each wants to know his thing entirely. Many succeed, some only in part; but the striving is in our nature. Well! Then seek infallibility where it is about life, where the prize is imperishable and is always granted to you in renewed beauty.

Do not confuse your life with the shimmer of it. What would you say of a mathematician who only had delight in the strangest geometric figures, but paid no attention to the necessity and the truth of them? Would you not call such a one a fool? Is it not just as foolish to wallow in the phenomena of life, but not seek the laws of it, and to not find in them the true, highest pleasure?

Where we see infallible truth, there we shall thank God who gave us the ability with which we are capable of recognising such things. It is not the truth which should delight us, but rather the gift of taking it up in ourselves by which we can raise ourselves to the infallible law and through that to immortality.

God is the eternal truth! He has given us of his light so that we shall separate ourselves from the darkness and live in his reflection.

God is everywhere, everywhere is truth, and humans are created for the recognition of God and for truth. We want to believe these principles, and connect ourselves with the eternal almighty so that we will prosper under his protection and arrive at immortality.

***

About the Author

Johann Baptist Krebs (1774–1851) was a renowned opera singer, director of operas, freemason, and esoteric writer who wrote under a number of pseudonyms (in particular, J. Kernning and J. Gneiding). He developed a form of letter mysticism composed of the concentrated thinking and feeling of letters through the parts of the body. This practice, described in part in this work, had its Biblical foundations described in depth in his student Karl Kolb's *The Rebirth, the Inner True Life, or How do Humans Become Blessed?* (also available from this publisher), and was further developed by Karl Weinfurter as well as being adapted by the founders of Runic Yoga.

www.ingramcontent.com/pod-product-compliance
Lightning Source LLC
Chambersburg PA
CBHW032302150426
43195CB00008BA/548